Country colour combinations

Country colour combinations

classic colour schemes that never fail

CAROLINE ATKINS

COLLINS & BROWN

First published in Great Britain in 2003
by Collins & Brown Limited
64 Brewery Road
London N7 9NT

www.chrysalisbooks.co.uk

A member of **Chrysalis** Books plc

9 8 7 6 5 4 3 2 1

British Library Cataloguing-in-Publication Data:
A catalogue record for this book is available from the British Library.

ISBN 1 84340 058 8

Project Editor: Gillian Haslam
Copy Editor: Alison Wormleighton
Designer: Christine Wood

Reproduction by Classicscan Pte Ltd
Printed and bound by Imago, Singapore
This book was typeset using ITC Berkeley, Neue Helvetica and Fineprint

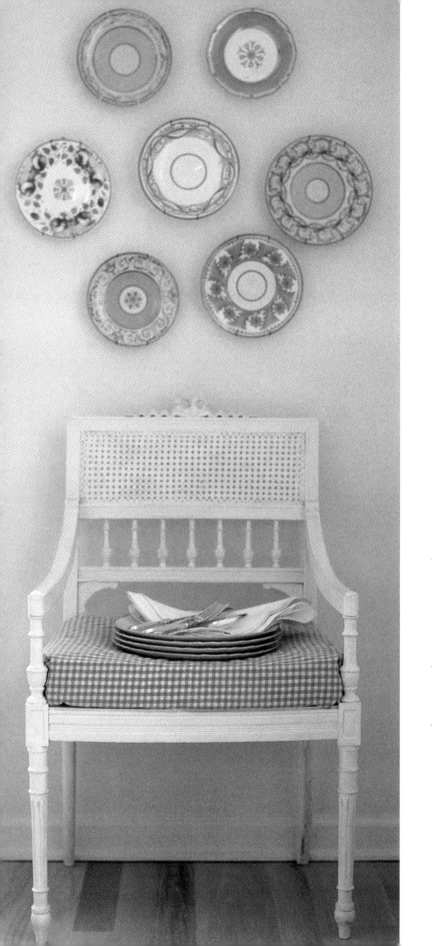

contents

foreword

by Susy Smith, Editor of Country Living Magazine

Welcome to *Country Living* Magazine's *Country Colour Combinations*, an irresistible palette of decorating schemes inspired by the natural shades of landscape and garden. *Country Living* features hundreds of houses furnished in imaginative detail and distinctive colours, and this book reflects some of their most versatile themes – the rich greens and golds of the hedgerow, the cool greys and blues of the coastline, the pastel blooms that fill country borders, the crisp hues of garden-grown fruits and vegetables, and the mellow neutrals of chalk, slate, stone and terracotta.

I hope you will enjoy decorating with these traditional colours, which celebrate *Country Living*'s philosophy of 'a timeless way of living'. For more practical advice and elegant inspiration for your home and garden, turn to the pages of our magazine every month.

Susy Smith

Glowing walls and paintwork, random-patterned cushions, and the natural tones of wood and stone combine in a 17th-century farmhouse to capture the glorious variety of country colours. The contrasts are rich and dramatic, the textures subtle, and the whole setting has a timeless sense of comfort.

introduction

Country decorating is full of classic colour combinations, some of them inspired by natural features such as flowers and foliage, others acquiring familiarity through traditional use – elegant blue and white china, crisp red and white gingham and the mellow green and cream dairy shades of old-fashioned kitchen larders. The best combinations are effortlessly comfortable to live with, because they are drawn from sources in which they sit side by side without jarring. This book demonstrates just why they work so well, showing you how to use them and also how to adapt them with subtle variations of your own.

Divided into five distinctive themes, it shows country rooms furnished and decorated in irresistible shades, along with sources of inspiration and practical information on how the colours influence each other, to help you recreate the effect for yourself. *Field & Hedgerow* captures the foliage, berries and meadow grasses of the changing seasons. *Sun, Sea & Sky* plays with the contrasting character of cool waters and summer warmth. *Flowers & Blossom* provides a rainbow of hues from country gardens and cottage borders. *Kitchen Garden* mixes fresh, crisp fruit and vegetable shades with the domestic traditions of a farmhouse kitchen. And *Slate & Stone* explores the subtleties and textures of natural materials which we sometimes take for granted, but which are in fact a treasure trove of elegant, restful furnishing colours.

As well as awakening your vision to the colour possibilities, textures and moods presented by different aspects of the countryside, each chapter begins with a palette of ten shades from which you can create your own decorating schemes. These form the basis for the rooms that follow, with further tints and tones being incorporated in each one to bring individual rooms to life, and contrasting accents showing how you can adapt them to suit different settings. The rooms themselves are full of natural inspiration, with selected combinations capturing specific country elements. Use them as your starting point, to give your furnishing schemes an outline structure, then experiment for yourself by drawing in colours from other themes and chapters. You'll find sympathies and similarities emerging – between the pretty pastels of the *Flowers* and *Sea* chapters, or the moody greys of *Sea* and *Slate*, or the fresh greens of *Hedgerow* and *Kitchen Garden*. Let these natural associations guide you from one palette to another, and you'll gradually acquire the confidence to mix and match between them.

FIELD & HEDGEROW

FIELD & HEDGEROW

GREENS, BROWNS, GOLDS AND TERRACOTTAS are traditional earth colours that appear naturally together in the countryside and are easy to live with in our homes. Their close affiliation is increased by the way the colours overlap through the seasons, appearing almost to contain one another as they shift from one shade to the next. Comfortable and relaxing, they work particularly well in sitting rooms, dining rooms and studies, where their warm tones create a familiar and inviting environment. Look for inspiration among the pale greeny golds of ripening cornfields and the bright golds of hay bales. Add splashes of berry red to the polished surfaces of dark brown or green leather furniture.

Right: Bright, glowing crab apples and crimson rosehips provide a flash of brilliant colour against the natural greens of hedgerow foliage.

Let rough, unfinished beams and floorboards recreate the mellow stripes of newly ploughed fields. Use soft, muted mushroom shades to provide gentle highlights and restful, neutral backgrounds, or in combination with warmer shades to cool them down. Experiment, too, with deep, dramatic purply blues – an unexpected shot of cool amid all this warmth, but perfectly reminiscent of hedgerow brambles and sloes. Enjoy the overwhelmingly natural effect that all these colours create as they intermingle, and reflect it by incorporating simple materials such as hand-thrown terracotta and earthenware, and including rough-woven linen and hessian among the rich, comfortable velvets.

field & hedgerow

THE FIELD & HEDGEROW PALETTE

These ten shades provide a basic palette for recreating the natural colours of the countryside. Use the stronger golds and russets for warm, autumnal settings, then add cooler, fresher accents with a range of greens, and occasional flashes of drama with bright reds and deep brambly blue-black. Pale yellows are restful as background colours, and neutral tones can be conjured up by the contrasting shades of soft mushroom or rich chestnut, depending on the effect you want. Let this palette inspire your initial colour scheme, then draw in other variations from the combinations shown on the following pages.

mushroom

The perfect balance to all the golds, greens and russets of the hedgerow. This soft taupe, cool but slightly pink-tinged, adds gentle contrasts against the richer shades, and also supplies its own very usable colour – the outdoor equivalent of coffee and cream. Try it in neutral, toned-down schemes, and look for fabrics such as linen and hessian that provide this versatile colour naturally.

wheat

The pale green-tinged yellow of the traditional cornfield. A muted gold with dark undertones, it can look subtly drab in quietly lit rooms, or merry and yellow in bright sunshine. This gentle, restful colour will add warm highlights to the rest of the palette and provide a mellow background for deeper tones.

hay

A brighter gold, full of sunshine and sparkle, that hovers between yellow and orange. Perfect for picking up the reflective highlights of gold paintwork and gilded picture frames, and also for creating a fresh contrast with bright greens and rich chestnut browns. A much hotter shade than wheat, it needs more careful handling, but is always warm and inviting.

lichen

A subtle and delicate silvery green that is incredibly useful – both as a cool, refreshing background shade, and to add soft highlights and details. Use it on woodwork as an alternative to white or cream, or to transform furniture with a coat of pale, Scandinavian-style colour. Make the most of its almost neutral quality in elegant combinations with taupes, greys and creams.

18

meadow

The fresh, bright green of spring and summer – far more energetic than pale lichen. An energizing colour to wake up to, it's good for bedrooms as well as being a refreshing shade for kitchens and bathrooms. Because of its leafy associations, it also makes a crisp, pretty mix with the blues, pinks and mauves from the Flowers & Blossom palette (page 76).

holly

A rich, glossy green with a distinctive sense of drama – perfect for formal dining rooms and book-lined studies. It is traditionally associated with winter, yet its evergreen character gives it a more durable quality than the rest of the palette: where the other colours shift and change according to the seasons, this green stays deep and atmospheric throughout the year.

russet

Pure autumn in a single shade. This is a classic country colour, reflecting the warmth of the traditional farmhouse kitchen, the changing shades of the seasons, and the natural character of materials such as wood, basketware and terracotta tiles. It mixes beautifully with reds and golds, and offsets fresher greens to perfection.

berry

A glowing, jewel-bright splash of pure colour amid the golden browns and yellow-greens of the hedgerow. Berry adds crisp, refreshing drama to the more muted greens, and also holds its own against the flame-tinged russets of autumn. Use it sparingly for accents and details until you feel confident with it, then try it for sumptuous, inviting dining and sitting rooms.

chestnut

The colour of conkers, polished wood and old leather, a rich dark brown that instantly sets a classic tone. Redolent of studies, libraries and gentlemen's clubs, it has a drama of its own, but is also very comfortable. Use it to add dramatic accents to lighter neutrals and bright reds and greens, and look for textures such as velvet and velour that match its luxurious depth.

blackberry

A blue-black purple that introduces a slightly different colour tone to the Field & Hedgerow palette. Dramatic but cool, it is remarkably versatile, providing effective contrasts to the brighter reds, greens and golds and also adding variety of texture, from the soft velvety blue of sloe and blueberry to the glossy, bead-like black of wild brambles.

Far left top: A collection of patchwork quilts incorporates the bright reds, greens, golds, russets and blue-blacks of the Field & Hedgerow palette and echoes the random mix in which they naturally appear. The painted cupboard reinforces the colours, with stencilled motifs in country style.

Far left bottom: A berry-red door and bright-painted hallway glow brilliantly against the rich, dark chestnut of a panelled wall and polished leather sofa. A russet and gold rug and the more muted shades of the faded linen cushion provide natural balance.

Left: Soft terracotta walls echo the warm tones of freshly turned earth. It's a gentle, powdery shade with plenty of texture, which suits rough-plastered surfaces and provides a restful background for the honey-coloured furniture and woven twig wreaths.

Above: Bright leaf green creates a dramatic background for pictures and statuary, reflecting the light to provide an atmospheric setting and a striking contrast with the reds and oranges of the kilim-covered chairs.

Above: Against a neutral background, muted terracotta and pale willow green have a natural, understated impact. The painted patterns on the planked cupboard are strong and graphic, but their Bloomsbury-style simplicity has a practical, utilitarian feel that suits both the functional kitchen setting and the natural quality of the colours.

Right: For a softer take on traditional autumn colours, offset the bright gold and faded russet of turning leaves with the pale silvery green of lichen. Painted tongue-and-groove panelling carries these colours beautifully, and coir matting adds natural texture.

Far right: Plain wood and natural basketware add their own colour and grain to a hedgerow colour scheme, toning down bright red and gold paints with a gentler, mellower touch.

Left: Contrasting greens conjure up the softness of early spring leaves, mixing pale and silvery shades with fresh and yellow-greens.

Right: Ochre walls create a wonderful background for the natural earth colours of gold and brown, as well as deeper flashes of russet and blueberry.

Far right: Billowing curtains in ripe gold, hand-painted with flowing lilies, frame this small-paned cottage window.

Below: Chunky earthenware, in shades from dark glazed brown to pale matt clay, mixes comfortably on a kitchen shelf.

Below right: The pale greeny gold of foliage creates a gentle contrast with terracotta pots and pinky purple flowerheads.

Below far right: This colourwashed wall layers russet over yellow, while the blind is striped in the colours of autumn leaves.

hay & russet

○ Look at an autumn forest to get the inspiration for your palette – collect leaves of different colours and press them to create a natural swatch board.

○ Mix different textures to reflect the variety of the hedgerow – rough linens, soft velvets, chalky paint finishes, twiggy baskets.

○ The Hay & Russet palette is rich enough not to need accenting, but you could cool it down with soft mushroom or offset the orangey red with a touch of contrasting green to represent a patch of summer foliage that hasn't yet turned.

○ Combine the two colours in a single colourwashed wall, layering russet on top of hay so that flashes of gold gleam through the darker surface.

Of all the glowing shades in the harvest palette, nothing captures the changing seasons of the country calendar like this glorious evocation of golden hayfields and autumn leaves. Suggesting the warmth of the late summer sun as well as the turning colours of the trees and hedgerows, it has a natural harmony that invites you in and makes you instantly comfortable. Here, cushions, covers, wood tones and paint shades all work together as easily as the foliage of an autumn forest. Contrasting textures will help to enrich the mix, so combine polished wood furniture with simpler, waxed finishes; deep velvets with thick, slubby linens and soft wool fabrics; smooth matt eggshell woodwork with the layered paintwork of colourwashed walls. To bring out the simpler elements of the harvest theme, add unglazed earthenware, painted wood accessories, woven baskets to hold logs and magazines, and dried grasses arranged in terracotta pitchers – furnishings that balance the glow of the colours with robust country practicality. This is a natural colour scheme, despite its intensity and drama, so enjoy playing with the different shades until you get the precise effect you want.

Left: Warm colourwashed walls and yellow painted ceiling beams are toned down by dado-height wood panelling and a striped throw in a cooler, mushroomy shade (see overleaf for more details on using mushroom colours).

Right: A stack of cushions in different textures and harvest colours blends with the polished surface of a carved chair back.

russet & mushroom

○ Add natural accessories such as baskets, dried grasses and woven twig wreaths to tie in with the neutral mushroom tones.

○ Use the soft mushroom to add muted accents to stronger colours without creating harsh contrasts.

○ Look for natural fabrics to carry the colour – linens, muslin, hessian and jute or coir floor coverings.

○ Mix different textures to give the limited palette more interest, adding rough-surfaced wood and including a few unglazed tiles among the glazed ones on a wall or worktop.

The pinky beige of field mushrooms has a cool elegance that perfectly balances the bright, burnished shades of autumn. Quiet and muted, it calms down the stronger colours, providing a neutral contrast far gentler than pure white. Whereas white details can be harsh and unforgiving, this soft taupe takes the heat out of warm russet, its subtle accents blending with the red tones rather than highlighting their difference. To prevent the two shades from fighting, try to avoid using them in equal quantities where it's not clear which one has precedence. Use the russet for touches of robust colour in a room with predominantly neutral tones, or the mushroom to add cooling touches to a wall painted in bold russet. And bring out the natural texture of the mushroom colour by mixing different finishes such as loose linen weaves, hand-embroidered patterns, mother-of-pearl buttons and glazed ceramic tiles.

Right: Warm russet takes the clinical chill off a bathroom, and softens the strong lines of the timber beams, which could look stark against a paler colour. Contrasting paintwork and ceramic tiles in a muted mushroom shade provide a gentle balance.

Below left: Russet-coloured fabric scattered with faded flowerheads makes an elegant cushion cover when trimmed with a wide border of plain linen and a neat button fastening.

Below: This loose-fitting linen chair cover in pale mushroom has been embroidered with a flowing fern design to reinforce the natural hedgerow theme. The cushion adds a flash of brighter warmth to the faded colour scheme.

berry & holly leaf

Startling and dramatic, the contrast of bright red and deep green has a refreshing boldness that can be turned to very different effects, creating elegant formality if combined with traditional furniture or practical country style with simple fabrics and distressed paint finishes. The drama springs from the fact that the two shades respond to each other like opposites attracted. Each of the three primary colours has a natural pair in the colour made by mixing the other two primaries together: this 'complementary' colour acts as both balance and highlighter. So green, which is mixed from blue and yellow, cools down the rich warmth of the red, and at the same time throws it into sharper relief. It's the crisp combination of bright winter berries against glossy evergreen leaves, appearing rich and jewel-like in a season when so much of the landscape is fading into neutral.

Right: The foreground room, painted in deep green, creates a striking contrast with the bold red walls of the room beyond. Soft white paintwork and graceful antique furniture and artefacts highlight the elegant architectural lines.

Below: Fresh red and white checks and an old green-painted bench show the colour combination in a simpler, less formal light, reflecting the natural leaf and berry associations of the two shades.

○ Play with the strong contrast of these complementary colours by using them in adjoining rooms to give the view greater depth.

○ Vary the effect by mixing them with polished wood and Regency stripes for formal elegance, or incorporating them in simple paintwork and nursery checks for a more casual look.

○ Look for polished or burnished surfaces such as green or red leather chairs and desktops to recreate the glossy finish of leaves and berries.

○ Offset the rich colours with white paintwork to create the wintry look of frost on holly.

wheat, hay & meadow

Below: Old green enamel mellows the gold of this kitchen.

Below right: A softer yellow provides the background for painted green furniture and a natural linen-covered chair.

The greens and golds of the summer countryside are a joyous, life-affirming mixture that translates brilliantly into furnishing colour schemes and provides surprising variety within its palette. The beauty of this combination is its sun-filled quality. Yellow, whether intense and glowing or pale and buttery, has an infectiously cheerful nature that lights up everything it touches, while the green of summer foliage and meadow grasses sounds a fresher, softer note. How you use the two colours depends on whether you want them to blend or contrast. Rich yellows, accented with touches of gilt in paintwork or picture frames, will work in harmony with mid-greens – especially if the green is used for a polished surface such as glass or enamel so that it reflects the gleam of the gold. Soft yellows, like pale corn, will provide a gentle background for stronger, deeper greens without the two shades fighting for attention. Think of the way fields are edged by darker borders of hedgerow foliage. Layer contrasting greens and yellows together, offsetting their brightness with patches of cooler, neutral colour – a plain covered chair, a set of linen curtains – so that you introduce a sense of how they fade naturally in the countryside. These are warm, inviting shades that fill the gloomiest corner with sunshine, creating welcoming hallways, light-reflecting garden rooms, and the sort of kitchen that everyone will want to spend time in.

○ Yellow is a strong colour to work with, but if you mix different yellows together they will temper each other's character.

○ Introduce neutral mushroom and oatmeal shades to tone yellows down further and calm the energy of brighter shades.

○ To bring out the richer tones of the yellow, add touches of gilding, such as ornamental mirror and picture frames, gold-leaf patterning on walls and furniture, or little gold-painted tables and chairs.

○ Include plenty of plants and foliage to add natural greenery to the scheme and maintain a sense of growth and regeneration.

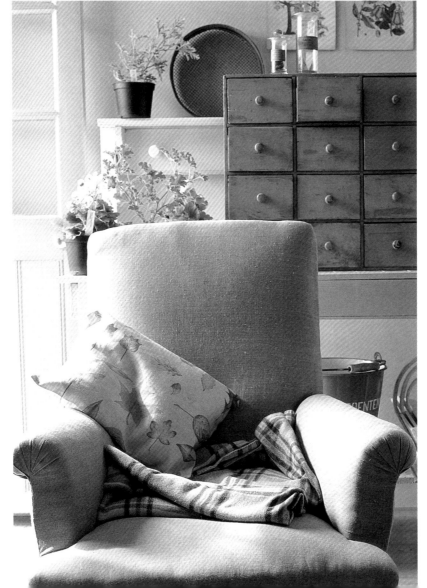

chestnut & copper beech

The woodland combination of textured bark, polished chestnuts and burnished copper beech leaves is irresistibly deep and rich. Moodier than the bright autumn shades, these colours have a more sombre look that lifts them out of the traditionally rustic and lets you use them in starker, more contemporary settings, creating sleekly sophisticated effects. Nutshells and copper beech trees share a delightful quality of variegated colour, providing subtly contrasting shades within their deep brown surfaces. In chestnuts, this can create a layered, almost colourwashed effect – as though they had been polished over the years like well-worn leather, smooth and glossy with some areas stained darker than others. On copper beech trees, the leaves themselves may change with startling splendour from mahogany to bright copper as the sap dwindles through summer and autumn.

To make the most of the colours in this palette, let these shades provide their own natural contrasts

○ Use textures to echo the effect of the colours – polished wood and leather contrasting with soft tweedy throws and blankets.

○ Use plaids and patterns for a more homely effect, and plain fabrics for elegance and drama.

○ Accent the browns with yellows and ochres to create a warm, mellow setting, or with whites and greys to keep the look cool and sophisticated.

○ Experiment with the palette, introducing 'transitional' shades to the pure red and brown for a more informal look.

○ Combine the warmest shades in sitting rooms and studies, or try a cooler mix for a relaxing bedroom.

Below left: Dark wood reinforces this room's mixed reds and browns.

Below: Polished wood glows against the brighter, coppery shade of the wall.

Below right: A flash of red adds instant drama to these neutral browns, whites and greys.

among your furnishings. The direction you take depends on the proportions you use of each colour, and the shades you pick to add the room's accents and highlights. The brighter, red-based tones will be a dramatic background for formal, polished furniture and gilt-framed pictures. Darker, more solid browns echo the beams and traditional woodwork of rustic style, so you can emphasize this with unpainted doors and dark-stained floorboards. If you pick up the transitional shades in warm, textured fabrics such as plaids and blanket-weave,

you will continue the cottagey theme as well as providing contrast to the smoother surface of the wood, and highlights of gold and yellow will give the whole effect a mellow autumnal feel. For a completely different look, use touches of dark chestnut brown and flashes of brighter copper to accent a more neutral scheme, and you have an altogether more contemporary style: crisp whites and muted greys are cool and wintry, and the introduction of a few layers of rich nut shades gives the room a sense of real drama.

moss & lichen

○ Use this soft, restrained palette to echo garden shades in muted tones, exchanging bright yellow leaf colours for nearly neutral greens.

○ Look for pale silvery green paints to maximize gentle light reflection and make small rooms feel larger and brighter.

○ Combine light and dark shades to create subtle contrasts and accent woodwork and architraves.

These delicate shades are a godsend when you want colour to be very subtle but not totally neutral. Whereas most pastels conjure up sherbet flavours or cottage-garden flowers, the organic character of green takes it closer to neutral creams, taupes and greys – naturally muted yet still with its own distinctive colour quality. Pale and elegant, soft greens set the tone for restful sitting rooms, tranquil bedrooms and cool, Scandinavian-style dining rooms. Especially effective in rooms that overlook gardens, they will reflect the haze of nearby foliage and bring a sense of the outdoor world inside. But this isn't the fresh, bright green of spring leaves: it's the subtle, silvery bloom you find where patches of lichen highlight textured bark and old stone walls, combined with the deeper tones of gentle, velvety moss. Use the darker shades

for mellow woodwork as the backdrop to comfortable scroll-armed sofas and faded tapestry rugs. Make the most of the paler, light-reflective colours for painted wooden furniture in graceful shapes to recreate an elegant setting reminiscent of traditional Gustavian style, shifting to slightly darker, earthier shades to accent occasional pieces and architectural details.

The natural quality of this palette makes it easy to adapt from old-fashioned florals to simple country patterns, so you can transform your look totally by incorporating different fabrics into the scheme: chintzy pink roses and trailing foliage for a traditional country-house sitting room; or Shaker-style checks in grey-greens for a simpler study or breakfast room, echoed by arrangements of lavender, rosemary and eucalyptus leaves.

Above: The bright green checked blind echoes the foliage outside and illuminates the more muted grey-green of the panelling.

Left: Subdued moss green paintwork contrasts with the paler walls of this sitting room and picks out the foliage in the faded fabrics and carpets.

Right: Walls and furniture painted in shades of soft, silvery lichen are accented by deeper grey-green accents and the dark blue-green of decorative foliage.

cornfield & ploughed earth

The pale gold of summer cornfields is a fabulous background for country furnishings – warm and sunny, but not too aggressively yellow. Combine it with sombre earthy browns and dark wood, and you recreate the contrast of adjacent fields, some thick with corn, others ploughed into stripes of newly turned earth. Rough-textured wood and uneven beams carry these darker colours very eloquently, while the paler yellow can turn up in the muted shades of flaking stonework and fading limewashed walls.

To make the most of the cornfield theme, look for chunky, rustic-style furniture that reinforces the sense of the country as a working environment, such as artisan-made, solid square chests and tables, and plain planked doors with blacksmith-forged latches and hinges. Or give the colours a more elegant interpretation by translating them into lighter, more graceful painted furniture and miniature pieces, decorated with stencilled details or delicate marquetry patterns. These daintier designs are perfect for introducing woods and veneers with paler finishes and intriguing grains – like walnut, burr elm and fruitwoods – and for showing off ornamental surfaces such as the age-distressed effect of craquelure. Whereas robust furnishings go best with simple coir matting and rush-seated chairs, you can combine elegant little carved side tables and turned-wood chairs with pretty needlepoint and embroidered fabrics in faded colours.

Left: The classic country colours of pale corn, ploughed fields and textured bark translate naturally into mellow schemes with rough-plastered walls, uneven beams and chunky unfinished wood.

Right: The same shades create a more delicate effect when used for painted wood and elegant marquetry patterns.

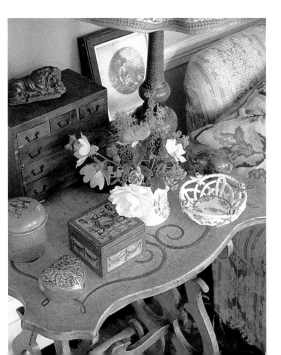

○ Yellow paint shades can be very tricky to get right, so look for unusual surfaces providing natural pale yellow tones, such as old flagstone floors and rush matting.

○ Accent the yellows and browns with touches of coppery red. Think of the richer tones of clay soil and introduce them in pictures and accessories.

○ In simpler, more rustic settings, you can echo the natural colour scheme with a jug of dried grasses or tall, dark-tipped bulrushes. If you opt for a more elegant furnishing style, try pretty meadow flowers, mixing in a few contrasting shades among the yellow.

○ The beauty of this palette is its natural quality, so echo the earthy, mellow tones with distressed or weathered surfaces that look as though they've seen plenty of use.

rosehip & crab apple

The beautiful, flame-toned skin of the wild apple, glossy but slightly rough-textured, seems to hold layers of colour beneath its surface, almost like paint glaze splitting to reveal another shade and then another under that. Crimson-pink bleeds into russet-orange and paler yellow, providing an entire palette of inspiration within a single fruit. Smaller than the cultivated apple, almost more like a large berry, it has the same quality of dense, compressed energy as the clusters of rosehips that form along the hedgerows when the summer blooms disappear into autumn. Use these bright, glowing colours to create striking schemes in which the different shades spark off one another: try placing hot-pink furnishings against a burnished orange wall, or a flame-toned cushion against a crimson chair. For a strong, slightly contemporary look, set confident blocks of colour against one another – one wall in gold, another in orange, a door in crimson, or perhaps a chest with different drawers painted in contrasting shades. Another idea is to paint the insides of cupboards in these colours. Emphasize the pink element for a crisp, berry-coloured effect, or the earthier orange tones for something more muted and Shaker-style, using terracotta tiles and pottery to draw out their practical, unadorned quality.

Left: Contrasting walls in crab-apple shades of yellow and russet create a strong background for the deeper red of the leather-seated chair and the simple painted box beneath the table.

Right: A flame-coloured cushion glows bright against the crimson wall and sofa, while the cooler, faded orange of the wall above the doorway adds another layer of gentle warmth.

❍ Be confident about layering colours one on top of another: these warm, glowing shades will lift and highlight each other rather than clashing.

❍ Use displays of fruit and berries to echo your decorating colours: as well as sprays of country crab apple and rosehip, you can add little potted orange and lemon trees for a more exotic use of the same palette.

❍ If the spicy shades feel too hot for comfort, introduce cooler elements to balance them: muted blue-grey slate will offset fiery orange tones, while touches of deep green or jet black will calm down bright rosehip pink.

❍ Let the warmth of these colours enrich rooms that don't get much natural light, and rooms that are designed for entertaining.

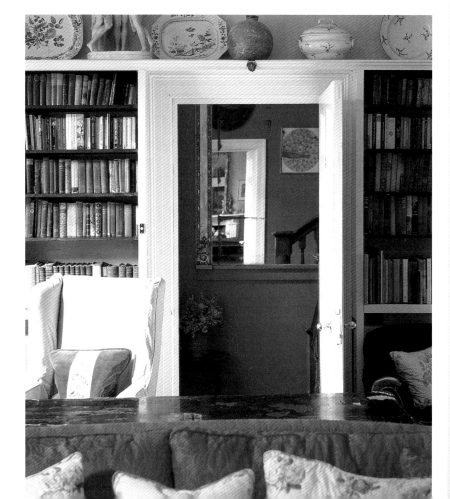

sloe & blackberry

- ❍ Use flashes of moody purple to create a sense of drama by enlivening softer colours or sobering up brighter ones.

- ❍ Enjoy the warm/cool contrasts of deep earthy browns and smoky blue berries, letting the shades offset one another in sleek sophistication.

- ❍ Look for surfaces that echo the skins of the different fruits – polished finishes that catch the light like glossy blackberries, or matt velvets with the soft bloom of sloes and blueberries.

- ❍ Explore the subtle variations of the fruit shades and find materials that match it, such as dark purple-brown leather furniture and suitcases, smooth ebony furniture or black lacquered dishes.

The deeper colours of autumn lanes suggest a different hedgerow colour scheme altogether. These are the shades that start to emerge against the bright jungle of summer foliage as the seasons change – blackberries darkening from red to purple, silvery blue sloes developing a velvety bloom. Heady and rich with the warming flavours of home-made wine and fruit preserves, they at the same time introduce a sense of coolness to the palette, the hazy blue and jet black adding a crisper, more wintry feel than the familiar golds and russets. One of the most effective ways to use these striking shades is to mix them into warmer schemes, creating moody contrasts between the colours or letting them draw on each other's different characters. Chestnut browns will contrast boldly with silvery blue. On glossy surfaces such as polished leather or glazed earthenware they can also reflect some of the cooler colour so that they take on their own, almost purple tinge, like fine chocolate. A dark purple cushion tossed in among warm russets and deep browns will create the same kind of brambly mixture that you see at blackberry time, when the turning leaves herald the new season. Use comforting winter fabrics such as knitted wool and soft velvet to echo their rich tones.

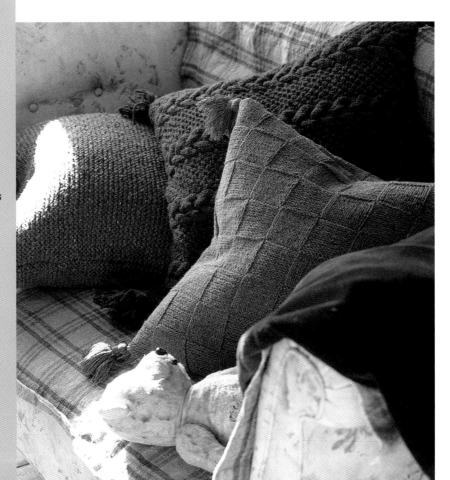

Left: A collection of knitted cushions in brambly purple-browns and rich autumn colours creates an inviting mix on a faded old sofa.

Right: Glazed earthenware in deep browns and blues picks up the colours of the table linen and reflects a glossy purple richness.

SUN, SEA & SKY

SUN, SEA & SKY

THE SEASIDE HAS ITS OWN UNIQUE CHARACTER. Of all the impressions evoked by country settings, this is the place to start nostalgic tingles and holiday excitement coursing through you, suggesting summer and free-dom, far horizons and unbroken sky. It has long been a source of materials and inspiration for decorating houses. Nautical striped fabrics, plain sailcloth and curtain headings lashed with rope or cord lend rooms a practical, functional feel. Model boats and lighthouses provide cheerful decoration for bathrooms and children's rooms. The soft, weathered honeys and greys of driftwood make attractive picture and mirror frames, while sea-polished pebbles and pearlescent shells have a natural beauty that has graced innumerable display shelves and dressing tables. This chapter explores all the subtle variations of tone and texture associated with seaside colours. The sea itself provides a palette incorporating greens, blues and greys of all shades, from the palest translucent aquamarine to deep inky blue-black. Pink and golden sand, bleached white chalk, rainbow pebbles and purple mudflats are set against a range of sky shades: from pure cerulean blue, to the rose and coral streaks that pierce the sky when the sun is setting, and the deep pewter of heavy storm clouds.

Right: The contrasting colours of the seaside include the pale blue of summer skies and the bright red of beach toys and striped lifebuoys. Cheerful and practical, these are shades that mix happily together and conjure up a relaxed mood of freedom and holidays.

THE SUN, SEA & SKY PALETTE

These ten shades provide a basic palette for recreating the natural colours of the shoreline. Concentrate on cool blues and aquas to conjure up a fresh, watery feel, or head for the yellows and pinks if you want warmer, sunnier tones. Mixing the two together will create bright, energetic contrasts and a very summery look, while introducing subtler shades of grey and off-white will calm the effect down and provide a softer, more restful setting. Let this palette inspire your initial colour scheme, then draw in other variations from the combinations shown on the following pages.

chalk

A cool, powdery white that provides clean, fresh accents against blues, greens and yellows, and creates a neutral background without the harsh glare sometimes associated with brighter whites. It works particularly well on uneven or textured surfaces such as rough-plastered walls and wood panelling, which bring out its chalky highlights.

coral

A glowing pink that adds a warmer tinge to cool seaside blues and greens, and introduces a touch of unexpected colour to the palette. Reminiscent of shell shades and the sky at sunset, it has a softer, prettier feel, more like the Flowers & Blossom palette, and enables you to create more varied effects than the fresh, watery tones of this palette usually permit.

sand

The pale yellow of childhood holiday beaches, warm but not overpoweringly hot, so that at its softest it is almost neutral. Sand is an excellent background colour for living areas, where it is comfortable and inviting without making too strong a statement. It also mixes beautifully with most blues and contains just enough yellow to throw whites and creams into sharp contrast.

sunshine

A brighter, hotter yellow, with a stimulating, energetic quality. Cheerful and glowing, this is a colour that really warms things up. It is a brilliant alternative to sunlight in small-windowed or north-facing rooms that don't get much natural illumination. It's not remotely subtle but can be great fun to use. Try it in the kitchen or playroom or to take the chill off a gloomy bathroom.

aqua

A wonderfully soothing, refreshing colour, perfect for bathrooms and bedrooms. So pale that it's almost translucent, aqua has a light-reflective quality that means it is an excellent space-maker, good for opening up small rooms. The cool, watery tone provides an intriguing contrast both with warm sunny yellows and with the rosier, pink-tinged colours of coral and coastal flowers.

sky blue

The classic pale blue of Regency drawing rooms and a perennial favourite for kitchens and bathrooms. Light and clear, it's almost endlessly usable – a safe choice and very easy to live with. The perfect wall colour to cool down over-bright rooms, it's also a good space-maker, and creates fresh, uncomplicated combinations with yellows, greens, pinks and deeper, stronger blues.

rockpool

A subtle alternative to the luminous glow of aqua. This grey-green shade has something of the muted practicality of traditional Shaker colours, although its character is liquid rather than earthy. Mix it with blues, greys, aquas and chalk white, letting its cool, intangible quality add depth and interest to the purer colours in this palette.

caribbean bay

Bright and dramatic – a colour that makes an instant impact and never lets you forget it's there. It's not for the faint-hearted, but is highly energizing if you have the courage to use it and is a brilliant way to conjure up atmosphere. Vibrant and slightly exotic, it pushes the natural shades of sun, sea and sky to their most extreme, so that you can almost feel the tropical heat.

azure

A warmer, richer blue for when you want stronger contrasts or a brighter background. This is the shade that can hold its own against dramatic Caribbean colours, as well as creating bold accents against glowing sunny yellows. Fresh and lively, it has a simple quality that feels practical enough to use in kitchens and children's rooms.

storm

The deeper tone that emerges when the blues of sky and sea lose their sparkle. Moody and cool, this adds stronger accents and lets you vary the pace of the brighter, fresher colours. It can supply drama where you need it, but it also has a neutral tranquillity and a close affinity with the pale green of sea and rockpools, making it a soothing contrast to bold blues and yellows.

49

Left: Sunshine streams down this yellow-painted hallway, reflected by the walls and cooled by the soft grey-blue of the woodwork. Bold striped rugs and plain wood furniture add a practical, nautical air.

Above: Clear sky blue creates a background for brighter, Caribbean-style turquoise tableware and sunshine-yellow flowers in this simple dining room.

Above right: The colour-washed finish of the walls gives them a faded, sun-bleached look, matched by the driftwood effect of the old weathered beams. Touches of blue add contrast.

Right: Sea green is cool and restful enough to employ in abundance — here, it is used for the panelled wall as well as the painted chairs and striped curtains.

Far left: The huge mop-heads of pale green guelder roses seem almost translucent against a background of blue-painted panelling, with touches of bright aqua and azure adding highlights.

Middle left: This pair of painted wooden chairs is chalk white against a wall of very pale sand and the sky-blue door. A clutch of yellow narcissi adds a burst of sunshine.

Left: The colours of white cottonwool clouds in a blue summer sky are perfect for the paintwork and tiles of this little bathroom. The cool and refreshing scheme is accented with a grass-green towel rack.

Below left: Deeper shades of blue and green create the moodier feel of the sea at night or in stormy weather, with the dark grey of the floor adding sombre shadows.

Below: Clear blue walls have a classic elegance, here stippled to give a watery, colourwashed effect. Cool and light-reflective, they are the perfect background for the mellow stone fireplace.

Far left: Cheerful checks and stripes conjure up the simple practicality of seaside style as well as its colours. White-painted panelling continues the beachhouse theme, with little coloured lanterns providing a decorative version of traditional nautical lighting.

Left: Use seaside memorabilia and beachcombing finds to reinforce the story. Little painted boats are perfect decoration for bathrooms and children's rooms, with shells, starfish and even dried seaweed strands providing unusual accessories.

Below left: Seaside colours work just as well in inland country settings. Use a pale sandy background for a gentle, restful atmosphere, adding painted blue-green woodwork and fabrics in subtle shades of pebble and driftwood.

Right: The combination of bleached wood and painted panelling is instantly shipshape, with drawstring bags adding neat nautical storage on the practical peg rail.

sky & sunshine

The brightest of the seaside colour schemes is also one of the most irresistible, rich with childhood memories of how summer ought to be. Perhaps the sun wasn't always that bright, or the sky so cloudlessly blue, but this joyous combination will make up for it, flooding rooms with sunlight and creating a sense of instant holiday. It's the simplicity that makes it such a good scheme for children's rooms: bright and stimulating, and with shades that seem perfect in simple fabric patterns like gingham checks and candy stripes. But it's well suited to the rest of the house too: cheerful and welcoming in a hallway, merry and fresh in a sitting room. The only thing you need to watch is the balance between the two shades. Think about which one is going to be your major colour, because this will establish the mood of the room. A predominantly yellow background with touches of blue will be warm and restful; reverse that with a blue-painted room furnished with flashes of yellow, and the atmosphere becomes cooler and fresher. White accents will offset either scheme with clean, crisp highlights, so aim for white woodwork and simple, white-painted furniture. A few pieces of natural wood and stone can be used to soften the sharp contrasts if needed.

○ It's hard to go wrong with blue and yellow, so use the colours with confidence and let the sunny mix add freshness and light.

○ Look for simple fabric patterns that reflect the practical colours: nautical stripes will combine well with schoolroom checks and bright plain cottons.

○ Use the combination in kitchens, children's rooms, sun-filled sitting rooms and chilly bathrooms.

○ Add splashes of different colours for accessories and other details.

Far left: This gentle, sunny wall is warm and glowing against the pale sky-blue paintwork of the door. Splashes of beachball red in flowers and accessories brighten up the setting.

Left: Yellow checks add zesty freshness to this little blue sitting room, offsetting the cooler walls with crisp colour.

Right: A yellow rose and natural pebble tones warm up the cool sky blue of the wall.

chalk & sky

The fresh, crisp mix of blue and white is a classic colour scheme. Though especially appropriate for kitchens and bathrooms, it is perfect almost everywhere, from practical children's rooms, to checked country sitting rooms, to elegant dining room china cabinets. At its simplest, it looks completely at home on painted woodwork, where the natural shadows of panelling and architraving coax tonal depth out of a single colour. Pale sky blue acquires deeper accents of grey and ultramarine, while chalk white lends itself particularly well to broken or distressed paintwork that highlights the powdery quality of its colour. Try plain whitewashed or limed wood, too, to create a similar effect of weathering or sun-bleaching. Painted floors and furniture respond well to these shades, and exterior weatherboarding, traditionally in white, can be painted blue for an instant seaside feel. This simple mix barely needs accessorizing with other colours, but clean reds, pinks and yellows will all add beach-bright accents, and touches of fresh green are reminiscent of a stretch of clifftop grass separating chalk and sky.

Left: Blue painted weatherboarding and flaking white woodwork create the sky and chalk mix at this beachside house. The shingle garden adds warmer tones of gold and coral as well as bright flowerheads.

Right: The white-painted linen press and chair create a crisp contrast with their blue background. The simple colour scheme effectively highlights the accents of the woodwork, from the planked floor to the carved detailing around the top of the cupboard.

○ Take inspiration from the way mismatched blue and white china mixes on a kitchen dresser – the different shades and patterns blend together because of the white background and glazed surfaces that they have in common.

○ Add warmer neutrals and natural accessories to offset the chill of the main colours. Pebbles, shells, basketware and coir matting will all work well.

○ Use painted wood furniture if possible. Any natural wood should be pale, stripped, bleached or limed – aim for the soft, textured effect of driftwood rather than dark, polished surfaces.

59

aqua & azure

If you had any lingering doubts about the wisdom of using blue and green together, these clear, liquid colours are the ones to change your mind. Shades of sky, from the pale blue of very early morning to the bright, cloudless expanse of high summer, blend beautifully with turquoise and aqua greens. Gentle and luminous, they work particularly well in soft paint finishes – think of the slight sheen on furniture or panelling painted in eggshell catching the light like sun on water, while faded colourwashed effects reflect both the translucence of water and the heat of the sun. Layer close shades of blue and green one on top of another and enjoy the tranquillity of their cool, refreshing harmony.

Left: Faded blue paintwork gives a sun-bleached look to the panelling and chair, while the door and floorboards are painted a brighter, fresher shade of aqua green.

Below left: Wooden coathangers and other practical accessories painted in cool, watery colours create gentle contrasts and provide a chance to try out different toning shades.

Below right: Spotted fabrics, ceramics and wallpaper pick out the different shades of blue and echo the seaside simplicity of the colour scheme. The painted cabinet adds a note of translucent liquid green.

○ Use aqua and azure in kitchens and bathrooms, rooms whose natural associations with water link them inherently to these cool, refreshing colours.

○ Keep the colours pale and liquid, so the contrasts are gentle and the shades blend into one another as though dissolving in water.

○ Look for light-reflective or broken-colour surfaces that complement the sense of delicate, intangible colour. Distressed or colourwashed paintwork will suggest bleaching by the sun or weathering from sea spray. Materials like old-fashioned enamel and lustreware have an iridescent finish that catches and diffuses light.

○ Keep patterns understated. Striped towels and curtains can be echoed by the lines of simple wood panelling and planked cupboard doors, giving a traditional beachhouse feel.

61

rockpool & driftwood

The subtlest of all the coastal colours are the grey-greens that emerge when the sun is fading: the muted shades of shallow water that captures the last of the dwindling light and reveals the shadows of rocks and billowing weed beneath its surface. At their purest, these colours have the translucence of limestone rockpools, where the clear white of the stone shows through the water and intensifies its colour. Cool and still, these tranquil hues have something of the same effect as the Moss & Lichen shades shown on page 36 – they are so pale that they're almost neutral, but with just enough tone to provide their own character. Restful as a background, with deeper accents supplying essential line and definition, these colours are easy to use and comfortable to live with – the perfect decorating combination.

To emphasize their natural quality, mix them with limed or bleached wood furniture and picture frames – faded surfaces reminiscent of shoreline driftwood and salt-whitened timber. These gentle neutrals blend beautifully with pale greens, greys and blues, creating mellow colour schemes for rooms you will relax in.

Below left: Simple watercolour paintings in hazy shades of grey and green explore the subtleties of the rockpool palette. The brighter wood of the old printer's trays emphasizes just how muted the background colours are.

Right: The faded wooden frame of a director's chair sits alongside more colourful painted designs. The pale green is a gentle background for a collection of old pictures.

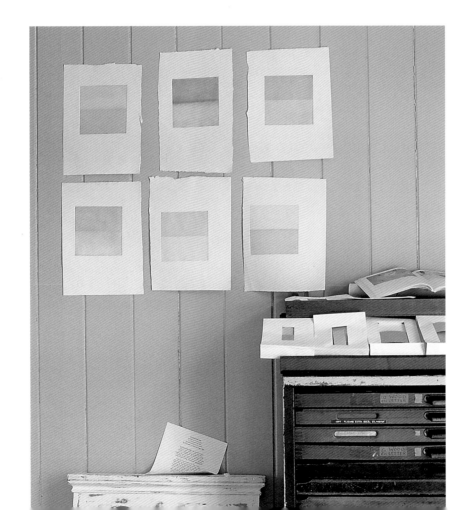

○ Use these shades as background colours, letting their soft, light-reflective quality provide restful calm.

○ Add furniture and accessories in darker greens and harmonious blues to bring out their deeper tones and create gentle contrast.

○ Add touches of brighter blue for sparkle – as though sunshine were highlighting these areas of the room.

○ Use chalk whites for occasional clean accents, so that the grey tones don't look muddy.

○ For moodier accents, add purply greys – the colour of mudflats, mussel shells and sea-washed pebbles.

caribbean seascape

○ These are bolder shades and it takes more courage to use them, but the risk is worth taking – after using them, you'll never be frightened of colour again.

In their most intense form, blues and greens take on a vivid, vibrant character that is saturated with colour. These are the sun-soaked shades of Caribbean beaches – colours that are generally too exotic for everyday use, but provide flashes of brilliance in unexpected places and a glorious way to enliven individual rooms and dark corners. In a bedroom, try the intense turquoise green of the Caribbean sea; it will glow extra-deep when lamplit by night, and will become almost translucent in the morning sun. Use the rich blue of a tropical night sky to turn a hallway into a room in its own right.

○ Try these shades in night-time rooms – sitting rooms used for evening entertaining, dining rooms and bedrooms – where they respond particularly well to atmosphere and candlelight.

Right: The deep blue of an evening sky, shot with lighter hues as though glowing in the moonlight, is cool and mysterious, a dramatic contrast against the bright green paintwork of the window seat.

○ Match their intense shades with splashes of accent colour or painted furniture in bright parrot reds and yellows: a scarlet vase or zesty lemon cushion will maintain the tropical holiday feel.

Below: Bright aqua floods an entire room with colour, so that it bounces off the wall and cupboard and tints the softer shades of the pictures and the painted chair.

○ For a mellower look, add weathered terracotta, the flaking, faded surface of which will provide a textured contrast with the rich colours.

shell, sky & sunset

○ This is the palette where the colours of the seaside overlap with those of the flowerbed, so it gives you a chance to introduce softer, prettier elements.

○ Pink provides a third primary colour but in diluted form, offsetting blues and yellows with a softer shade than bright red.

○ Touches of pink and coral will warm up blues and enrich yellows, or even make a simple blue background sharp and contemporary.

○ Introduce the colours in accessories, so that they don't dominate the setting or detract from the freshness of a blue or yellow scheme.

○ Look for authentic materials that will emphasize the quality of the colours: pinks and whites in iridescent surfaces such as lustreware and mother-of-pearl, blues and yellows in chalky Mediterranean paints.

The traditional blues and yellows of the coastline take on a new character if you also work pink into the mix, reflecting the pretty shades of shell and coral, the warm glow of a setting sun, and, in brighter flashes, the colours of seaside flowers like thrift and tamarisk. At its simplest, this could just mean setting a vase of pink blooms against a blue wall, but to integrate the colours more completely you could look for a fabric that incorporates all three in its pattern, or accessorize a predominantly blue and yellow room with cushions, rugs or china in shell pink. Weathered pink paintwork and raw plastered walls will evoke the layered, streaked effect of a sunset sky, and pale terracotta tiles will echo the soft pinky beige of sea-washed pebbles.

Left: Walls half-painted in a chalky pink terracotta add a glowing warmth to this yellow kitchen with its soft sky-blue woodwork.

Below: Flashes of deep pink, like blooms of thrift or the waving tentacles of sea anemones, are bold and dramatic against traditional blue-painted seaside panelling.

storm cloud & sea spray

○ Look for natural materials in the colours – a dish of grey and white pebbles on a windowsill, a slab of marble on a white-painted washstand, slate floors and worktops, and alabaster vases.

○ Monitor the level of colour carefully – don't let it get too blue or too green or you will lose the subtle anonymity of this intangible shade.

○ Keep the scheme alive with plenty of fresh white accents, otherwise the moody, sombre tone may start to feel oppressive.

○ Use it in bright, south-facing rooms that get plenty of sun and need calming down. These cooler tones will make the space more comfortable.

The sea has its darker moods, and the pewter grey of a threatening storm will add sombre colour that anchors light, fresh decorating schemes and gives them more impact. Reflecting hints of sea green and sky blue in its shadowy tone, it will provide a coolly dramatic background for painted furniture, pretty fabrics and displayed paintings. Use it with plenty of white, like the frothy waves of a storm-tossed sea, and the effect will be fresh and distinctive, the crisp contrast ensuring that the muted grey never becomes gloomy.

This is a colour scheme just made for bathrooms and kitchens, where it gives paintwork and panelling a simple, functional look. It is also effective in bedrooms, where its lack of obvious colour is quietly soothing, as though the light had been switched off to calm down the energetic glare of the sun. Choose your shade carefully, and it will have the stillness of Wedgwood blue, producing a deep, subtle background against which white paintwork and accents stand out like the classic cameos and silhouettes on a Wedgwood vase.

Left: Cool grey paintwork gives this bathroom a practical finish, calming down the brighter cobalt blue of the floor and echoing the darker touches of inky blue in the ceramics and shower curtain.

Right: A moody grey wall provides a dramatic background under the eaves of this attic bedroom, contrasting with the sloping white walls and pretty sprigged bedlinen.

○ Use these subtle, muted colours in simple, Shaker-style kitchens, as well as in sitting rooms – their quiet character makes them easy to live with.

○ Maintain the mellow feel of the room by opting for plain wood and natural floor coverings.

○ Add simple accessories and naive-style paintings that suit the faded colours and evoke childhood memories.

○ If you're worried about the colours starting to seem muddy, freshen the scheme by adding touches of white and cream.

sand & summer sky

The pale gold of a sandy beach – almost white when dry and bleached, darker where the tide has drenched it – brings back memories of childhood holidays. You can actually feel the grains between your toes, your feet shifting their hold as the water is squeezed out beneath them. Chalky, Mediterranean paint finishes recapture that texture, as do pigment-mixed limewashes, with colour that fades and surges in response to the amount of moisture in the walls. Best of all, it's a mellow, earthy colour that's restful to live with – richer than cream but still softer than the bright cheerfulness of sunshine yellow. Combine it with the old blue of painted boats, children's beach buckets and 1950s postcard skies, and you end up with a nostalgic scheme that's all the more evocative for its faded, muddy quality, as though it's been weathered by use. Not as bright or fresh as the Sky & Sunshine mix (see page 56), it has strong resemblances to the muted tones of Shaker style, and suits the same understated lines: simple furniture, painted floorboards and plain woodwork reminiscent of nautical decking.

Left: Simple Shaker lines give this sitting room a restrained, old-fashioned look, with muddy-blue paintwork and plain wood against whitewashed floorboards and pale, sand-coloured walls.

Right: Old enamel storage jars and plain checked curtains in a soft, muted blue add nostalgic colour against pale yellow walls.

FLOWERS & BLOSSOM

FLOWERS & BLOSSOM

THIS PASTEL PALETTE provides endless inspiration, with soft, sweet shades. Because of their similarity in tone, they can be intermingled in almost any combination without jarring – from the mixed rainbow of sweet peas to self-contained combinations such as pink tulip heads tinged with cream. Whether in fabric, wallpaper or paint colours, these blues, pinks, creams and mauves, juxtaposed with the pale green of summer foliage, conjure up the beauty of country gardens and cottage borders. Saturated with summer memories, the flowers suggest intriguing textures too, the contrasts between frothy blossom, velvety rose petals, tight-wrapped buds and frilly, pinked carnation heads providing the sort of variety you need in furnishings and finishes. Overlapping occasionally with Sun, Sea & Sky shades, and with the prettier end of the Kitchen Garden palette, they can be shot through with subtle highlights and will shift and change during their life. Hydrangeas can start off one colour and end up another; bright blue forget-me-nots can be flecked with pink; scarlet rosebuds streaked with yellow may become the palest pink when open. Full of surprises, never predictable, flowers also acquire a silvery pearlescence from early morning frost and dew, so look for enamel, mother-of-pearl and shimmering satins to add lustre to the colour.

Right: Fragile rose petals in soft pink tinged with gold capture the delicacy of the colours and textures inspired by the flowers of the garden border.

74

THE FLOWERS & BLOSSOM PALETTE

These ten shades provide a basic palette for recreating a gardenful of floral furnishing colours. Use the paler, pastel blues, pinks and mauves to devise restful, romantic schemes in bedrooms and sitting rooms, then add brighter, crisper accents with energetic spring hues, and touches of rich luxury with deep pinks, reds and purples. Incorporate plenty of fresh greens to supply an element of cool, leafy calm, and enjoy experimenting with these harmonious, nostalgic shades. Let this palette inspire your initial colour scheme, then draw in other variations on the same theme from the combinations shown on the following pages.

primrose

The pale yellow that appears in spring drifts along woodland banks and in shady gardens. Incredibly delicate, it's barely more than cream, so that its pure shade only comes through when used in quantity as a wall colour, or when highlighted by contrasting accents of pink or purple. Take a look at the Kitchen Garden palette (page 106) to find similar soft, milky shades.

alchemilla

A soft, yellowy green that can sometimes appear as one colour, sometimes as the other, depending on the accents with which you offset it. Fresh and cool, it works especially well in natural sunlight and has a glowing, reflective quality. Try using it with pale mauves, so that it echoes the traditional cottage garden combination of lady's mantle (alchemilla) and lavender.

cherry blossom

The pale pink that smothers trees in spring – very soft and versatile and not too sugary. An incredibly gentle, restful shade, it is traditionally used for babies' bedrooms but is equally suitable for bathrooms, sitting rooms and anywhere that you want a hint of warmth without feeling overwhelmed by colour. If you've never thought of yourself as a 'pink' person, this is the one to try.

lilac

A soft hazy shade, almost grey but with a pretty pastel tint to it. Beautifully tranquil and light-reflective, the colour of lilac blossom is fresh but soothing, its cool, calming nature creating the perfect background for bedrooms, bathrooms and sitting rooms. A distinctive alternative to blues and pinks, it mixes comfortably with the yellows and greens of the spring garden.

sweet pea

A full, strong pink that can hold its own against the dark purples and fuchsias of a mixed summer flowerbed. The fragility of the sweet-pea petals doesn't dilute this colour, so it is an extraordinary combination of vibrance and delicacy. It takes more courage to use, but is wonderful with fresh leafy greens and soft, creamy yellows, which cool down its lively tones.

peony

The deep colour of the traditional garden peony. A bold shade that hovers between red and pink, it is also found in the crimson-flushed tips of the softer, paler pink peony and in velvety, scented roses. Strong but not harsh, it's surprisingly easy to live with, adding rich, luxurious accents and mixing well with both floral pastels and earthier, faded colours.

forget-me-not

A clean, clear blue, cool as ice but full of summer sunshine. The classic shade for kitchens, bathrooms and baby boys' bedrooms, it also offers a refreshing way of toning down rooms that feel too bright. It has an intense quality despite its pastel paleness: the flowers glow from leafy flowerbeds like pinpricks of light. This translucence means the colour is a brilliant space-maker for small rooms.

bluebell

The purply blue that appears in spring and continues through summer in flowers such as grape hyacinth and agapanthus. Mauve in some lights, definitely blue in others, it is a shifting, intangible colour that fades gradually through a range of shades and blends beautifully with most blues and lilacs.

leaf

Much stronger and brighter than alchemilla, but still contributing a light, yellowy tone that always feels springlike. Fresh and energetic, it mixes quite comfortably with all the floral shades, but can also be used with the deeper, mellower greens of the Kitchen Garden (page 106) or to add a zesty crispness to the golds and russets of the Field & Hedgerow palette (page 18).

violet

Darker and moodier than lilac, and capable of more dramatic effects. Violet has the pretty colouring of the rest of the floral palette, but its deeper tones are more robust in comparison with the delicate pastels. Use it to create opulence and atmosphere and mix it with gilded accessories for a sense of luxury. If you feel wary of such a strong shade, try it out in small accents.

Left: Bunches of lilac, lavender and heather are hung upside down to air-dry in a rustic cloakroom. Green-painted tips on the old-fashioned peg rail echo the colours of the foliage.

Right: Bluebells are the stuff of fairytales – in folk legend, a child who picked them alone in the wood would never be seen again. These woodland flowers, which flourish in secluded, shady gardens, hold a lovely range of blue and mauve colours in their delicate bells.

Far right: Cool lilac and fresh forget-me-not blue are pretty and restful in a white-painted bedroom, with touches of cherry blossom pink adding a contrasting trim to the bed's drapery.

Below: The pinks and greens of a summer garden will inspire a host of paint colours, fabrics and accessories once you let your imagination loose.

Far left: Curtains patterned with moody violet flowers on a soft primrose background provide a dramatic flourish against a lighter, hazier, lilac-painted wall.

Left: Flower shades always work comfortably together, because even the strongest colours are often mixed in vases and borders. Here, wild bluebells and deep pink tulips create a romantic, cottage garden pairing.

Below left: Greens are a natural partner for floral colours, recalling the foliage that surrounds them in garden, meadow or woodland settings. The combination of green and purple is especially subtle, like borders of alchemilla and lavender spilling onto a cottage path.

Right: Neutral tones can be introduced to the floral mix too, a reminder that the blooms and foliage will gradually lose their colour and fade to pale gold and bleached straw.

Far left: Decorative paintwork gives you the chance to incorporate a range of complementary shades in a single room. These freehand designs, loosely worked on a backdrop of simple wooden panelling, combine stylized flowers and leaves with more graphic, abstract shapes, mixing greens, blues, yellows, pinks and lilacs in a pastel, summery haze.

Above left: Outdoor colour scheming can reflect garden shades too, with simple contrasts picking up the colours of flowers and foliage, as in this soft green-painted window frame against the chalky lilac wall of the house.

Above: The same combination of colours can be carried through to the bedroom, with touches of crisp white linen to add contrast.

Left: The smallest accessories will carry a colour scheme through to the last detail. A bathroom decorated in flower shades has plenty of scope for inspiration – from soft pastel paints to pretty towels and floral-patterned fabrics and wallpapers. Even the soaps and toiletries can be chosen to match.

83

forget-me-not & cherry blossom

The clear ice colour of forget-me-nots has a brighter quality than so many garden blues – pale but intense, so that they sparkle like clusters of pastel stars among the spring foliage. These tiny flowers, simple and sure of themselves, spread unbelievably fast, with a confidence that isn't shaken by their habit of turning pink in unexpected patches. It has the same simplicity of tone as its sister pastel, cherry blossom pink, which is why these two colours have provided the basis for generations of nursery furnishings – the traditional blue-for-a-boy, pink-for-a-girl mantra reflecting their uncomplicated nature. But their pure, gentle shades are equally restful in grown-ups' bedrooms, and in bathrooms and sitting rooms, where their straightforward prettiness has an easy, undiluted charm. Soft cashmere blankets and beribboned satin quilts provide this sweetest of combinations with plenty of contrasting texture, while light, floaty voile or organza curtains add a more whimsical, romantic touch. Sprigged floral prints, and patterns incorporating boughs of cherry blossom, are perfect for these settings and will also mix effortlessly with simple country checks and stripes, especially if you trim them with pretty bows and rosettes, and delicate fabrics such as lace and broderie anglaise. Be careful to keep the effect understated, however, with plenty of areas of plain colour, and crisp whites or soft creams to offset the pastels and prevent them from looking too sugary. Plain floorboards and light wood or painted furniture will reinforce the natural, unsophisticated feel.

○ If you want to add more depth of colour, introduce accents of lilac or slightly brighter sweet-pea shades.

○ Avoid using strong patterns that will swamp the delicacy of the colours, or fight with their purity. Keep it simple.

○ Vary the look of the room with natural wood for a rustic feel, or painted furniture and floorboards for a prettier, daintier look.

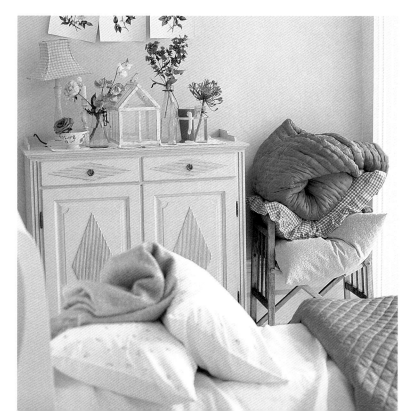

Far left: Pastel blue covers and pink checked curtains create a tranquil bedroom. The old-fashioned blankets striped in faded pinks and lilacs and simple second-hand furniture keep the effect practical rather than whimsical.

Left: Forget-me-not blue walls are matched by a blossom-pink blanket and soft quilts in deeper sweet-pea pastels.

Right: Ribbon ties add a pretty finish to a cherry-blossom pink cushion on a blue-painted garden chair.

lilac & primrose

○ Think of the combination of violets and primroses in Easter posies, and don't be afraid of using the two colours together: shades of purple, mixed from the primary colours of blue and red, are natural partners to yellow, the third primary colour, and will cool it down.

○ If the combination feels too strong, try it in a milder, less dramatic form by softening lilac into grey or yellow into cream. You will still have the warm–cool balance of colours.

○ Don't feel you have to mix large areas of solid colour: a lilac cushion on a yellow sofa will provide an effective accent, and a single fabric will happily combine floral sprigs in both shades.

○ If you let the colours get darker and moodier, it will still be an effective combination, but you will lose the fresh, spring appeal of the lighter shades.

The sweet, pastel nature of some floral shades makes them almost edible, and yellows and mauves are among the most delicious, evoking the colours of sugared almonds and those little iced rosettes found on old-fashioned biscuits and handmade Easter eggs. Even without its fragrance, the colour of so many scented blooms – lilac, lavender, violets, wild thyme – is powerfully atmospheric and adds a wistful, slightly mysterious effect to decorating schemes. But combine it with fresh, merry yellow – whether pale, delicate primrose or the brighter gold of spring daffodils – and the mix is a heady one, full of interesting contrasts. The natural balance of warm yellow with cool lilac means they offset one another perfectly, tempering each other's strengths, while at the same time the essential character of each colour becomes more intense by their pairing. Try them together in a bedroom, where the combination of tranquil lilac to lull you to sleep and glowing yellow to wake you up adds up to the perfect blend. Or experiment with slightly stronger shades in a sitting room, setting deep amethyst glassware against a yellow wall, or finding a fabric that entwines the two.

Left: Painted on the upper and lower halves of a bedroom wall, the two contrasting colours balance one another, with paler gold and grey echoing their tones in the fabric of the chair.

Right: A small bowl of cow-parsley heads mixed with a few Canterbury bells sits next to an elegant lilac-banded tureen on this gingham tablecloth.

mixed hydrangeas

The shifting, unpredictable shades of old-fashioned hydrangea blooms are a lucky dip of decorating colour. Opening out from their multiple buds into petals of pale, creamy green, they gradually flood with colour like a child's 'magic painting' book – the sort with black and white pictures that come to life when you add water. But even then you can't be sure what colour will emerge. The most likely is a strong, rosy pink, or perhaps a darker carmine red. Certain types will turn a clear sky blue – but only if planted in acid soil: if the mix is too alkaline, the blue will give way to pink again. You'll also find creamy white varieties, and shop-bought blooms will give you even more choice, including deep mauves. You don't often see the different colours together in a domestic garden, because the soil will dictate that they go in one direction or the other, but their sweet, intense shades have a natural affinity that betrays their source as a single palette.

Draw inspiration not just from the colours but also from the shape of the blooms, and from the contrast between big pompom mop-head hydrangeas and the more delicate, feathery lace-cap varieties, which have a central filigree of tiny blossoms within their circle of larger flowers. Select different textures and patterns to reflect this variety – for example, setting soft, fluffy fabrics against intricate lace designs and wrought-iron decoration.

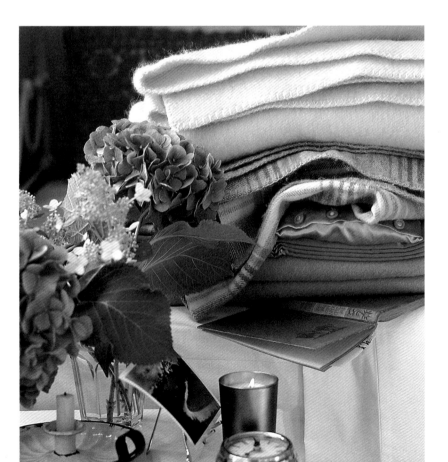

Far left: The painted surfaces of brickwork, furniture and floorboards combine to create an interior-style floral colour scheme on this outdoor terrace.

Left: A stack of soft blankets and satin pillowcases in hydrangea shades of pink and blue is accented by a vase of deeper purple blooms.

○ Remember how hydrangea colours shift and fade, and keep your decorating plans flexible. You can add or subtract any of these shades if you want to make subtle changes to the scheme.

○ Use the pale green of the early petals and the lace-cap buds to provide gentle accents and highlights in contrast to all the heady pinks and blues.

○ Let the old-fashioned romance of the flowers provide traditional colour schemes for bedrooms and sitting rooms.

bluebell & lilac

For a few weeks each year, the garden hovers between spring and summer, and the drifts of bluebells give way to early blooms of scented lilac. Hazy and mutable, the colours of both flowers are hard to pinpoint, however well we think we know them, and however widespread their use has become as identifying nametags for specific shades. Bluebells can be pink or white as well as blue, and lilac comes in a range of hues from white through pinks, mauves and reds to deepest purple. The clear blue and soft mauve varieties are the most familiar, and these are the colours that are easiest to live with, but even in these gentle shades you can see different tones providing depth and highlights. The blue fades from its initial spring intensity to a paler, luminous colour; the mauve blossom holds deeper shadows within its bell-like clusters. Together, these delicate colours, so similar in tone, create a combination of perfect freshness and tranquillity, mixing quietly in fabrics and decorating schemes that reflect their sweetness and bring a sense of the garden inside.

Left: The luminous blue of fading bluebells highlights the pretty decoration of this wrought-iron bed against the hazy, lilac-painted wall.

Right: The blues and mauves of these familiar garden blooms are mixed with harmonious pinks and touches of spring yellow. Soft white paintwork keeps the whole effect fresh and delicate.

○ Aim for similarity of tone, adding other harmonious pastel shades rather than strongly contrasting colours.

○ Look for sprigged and floral patterns featuring these flowers, and mix them with plains and checks for a simple, country-garden effect.

○ Keep the furniture light and elegant, with pale paintwork and graceful shapes such as carved wood and decorative wrought iron.

○ Add traditional accessories to match the old-fashioned colours – crystal chandeliers, dainty ceramics, scallop-edged lampshades and vintage patchwork quilts.

lavender & alchemilla

This is the most restful of all garden-flower combinations, a subtle haze of colour that stays beautifully understated. The pale green froth of alchemilla (or lady's mantle), one of those ambiguous plants whose blooms seem to be part of the foliage rather than separate flowerheads, is always cool and refreshing against all the harsher brights of a summer border. Its traditional pairing with lavender – alternate clumps of colour spilling onto either side of a garden path or lawn – is inspired. Their gentle natures make them two of the easiest shades to live with, and, used together, they create an irresistible sense of quiet calm. Natural mixers with pale woods and mellow basketware, they themselves fade beautifully into soft greys and neutrals. As well as paints, fabrics and ceramics, you will also find these shades in smoky-veined marble and lichen-covered stone. These materials can either be used as part of your furnishing scheme or left in a garden setting where their muted tones will look even more at home.

Right: An old bleached-wood cabinet and peg rail emphasize the muted colour scheme of green and mauve fabrics and ceramics, creating the effect of a faded photograph in this country cloakroom.

Far right: Layers of soft green and lilac, seen one beyond another as you look through these doorways, contribute softly contrasting tones to a scheme of washed-out country house colours.

❍ To keep the effect muted, combine lilacs and greens with materials and colours that emphasize their natural character – stone, grey, stripped wood or the faded terracotta of old garden pots and bricks.

❍ For a fresher, more obviously floral feel, add plenty of white accents in woodwork and linens.

❍ These colours will work almost everywhere, but are especially restful in settings such as bedrooms, sitting rooms and floral-themed bathrooms.

❍ Try them as an alternative to the more commonly seen combination of pink and green – using lilac instead of pink gives a cooler, subtler effect.

rose & peony

Almost from childhood, we learn to be wary of mixing such heady colours as pinks and reds. The warmth and overwhelming richness of the combination are enough to warn off most decorators – even without the risk that the resulting scheme might be a little less sophisticated than we were hoping for.

The secret of working with these colours, how-ever, is to have confidence. Trust in their natural toning contrasts to suggest harmonious shades that will sit comfortably together, and – with an even greater act of faith – take a lead from the vibrant colours that appear side by side in garden borders,

flower shops and bouquets. If you stopped to think about what you were doing, you might falter, but as long as you can envisage the glorious indulgence of velvety roses next to blowsy, full-petalled peonies you won't lose heart.

Your furnishing schemes don't need to be quite so rich, though. Take a single pale pink peony head and look for the deeper reds that bleed through it. All you need for a country dining room with a beautifully tranquil atmosphere is to use the pale shade as a background and pick up on the stronger tones for fabrics and ceramics, and the very deepest tones, dark purply-browns, for furniture.

❍ If the combination feels too strong, concentrate on the paler shades, adding plenty of white to cool the scheme down, and just a few darker accents.

❍ The bolder colours will create a more contemporary effect, so back them up with clean, streamlined shapes and a few pieces of modern furniture.

❍ Flashes of deep, bright pink – nearer fuchsia than rose – will add drama and energy when combined with more sugary shades.

❍ Remember that pinks and reds have a warming effect, so use them in rooms where you want to feel secure and enclosed.

Right: Traditional panelling adds contrasts and shadows to the pale pink paintwork, suggesting deeper tones that are then picked up in the chair fabric and the dark wood furniture.

Far right: Pink walls and woodwork create a rich, warm setting with a strong sense of drama. Accents of deep peony red keep the effect sharp rather than sugary.

lupin & foxglove

Standing tall in cottage garden borders, the pink and purple flower-clad spires of lupins and foxgloves add structure and elegance among plants with a looser, more rambling habit. They may be nominally 'wild', but their height and restraint create a natural sense of order, and their colours have an intensity that can't be ignored. Dark pinks and purples, moody and deep against garden foliage and enjoying the drama they bring to shady, woodland places, are individually striking and even more effective when used in combination. Rich and jewel-like, these are colours that conjure up luxury in the simplest setting, and provide a perfect balance between warm and cool. Use them for lustred materials like velvets, silks and iridescent metals and they will add instant opulence; try them in soft woollens and woven plaids, and the absorbent quality of the fabric will emphasize their more muted, shadowy tones.

   In some ways these are perfect evening colours, which will be brought to life in a candlelit dining room or a romantic bedroom. But their mutable nature, making the flowers equally at home in a sunny border or leafy corner, means that their pretty, feminine shades are also soft enough for bathrooms and sitting rooms.

Left: Delicate pink china acquires a dramatic look when accessorized with silk ribbon and enamelled silverware in a deeper, richer purple.

Right: Both pink and purple take on a muted shadowy tone when used for soft woollens, blankets and plaids, with floral pink details adding a fresher, more traditional touch.

❍ The balance between the two colours is the secret here, so don't be tempted to go with a single shade unless you want a very different effect. The pink is warmer and fresher, while the purple provides a deeper, moodier quality.

❍ Like all flower colours, the combination can be offset by small amounts of green to add some contrast and balance.

❍ This is probably too strong a mix to use for walls as well as furnishings, but it works beautifully if you add touches of pink and purple against a soft neutral background – creams and whites will keep the colours looking fresh.

❍ Add plenty of white-painted woodwork so that the deeper, moodier tones of the colours don't become muddy or dominant.

❍ Keep the colours pale and discreet, with no dramatic contrasts or bold accents.

❍ Use soft pastel shades to reinvent simple wooden and metal furniture. Painting them with a coat of eggshell colour will highlight interesting shapes and turn functional items into something much prettier.

❍ For cooler accents, introduce the occasional touch of ice blue. It isn't a colour found among stocks or sweet peas, but it has the same quality of tone and adds a refreshing crispness.

❍ Stronger accents can only be included if they are transparent or translucent – such as the green glass lamp base shown right. Dense colours will simply unbalance the scheme.

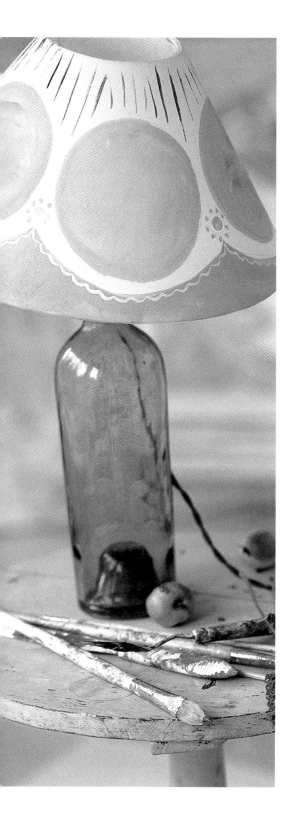

sweet peas & stocks

Pastels always mix more comfortably than other shades, and the beauty of a bed of sweet peas is the way random colours mingle together, their flimsy petals ruffled like tiny scraps of silk. There's sheer romance here, reminiscent of frilly party dresses, wedding cakes and sugared almonds. Pinks, mauves, creams and whites, with their long, slender, pale green leaves and trademark twining stems, create an irresistible palette of gentle decorating colour. Scented stocks contribute additional depth, with softly clustered blooms that look all the better for being mixed, several shades together, in vases and pitchers to make indoor displays. Use these delicate colours for paintwork and furnishings and you fill the house with year-round summer. Soft enough to provide gentle backgrounds as well as pretty fabrics and accessories, they are a wonderful combination of sweetness and subtlety, creating schemes that it's simply impossible to dislike.

The secret of their success is the barely-there colour. Think of the care with which you tint cake icing – adding the merest drop of deep red cochineal to turn the sugar mixture pale pink – and apply the same caution to all these shades. Start with as near to a pure white setting as you can get, then build up the pastel tones layer by layer, keeping them almost translucently pale and never letting the idea of 'colour' run wild and risk unbalancing the scheme. There's no need for pattern: blocks of plain pastels set against one another have just enough contrast for variety, and these pure colours have a simplicity and elegance that will carry the scheme without effort. Bedrooms, sitting rooms, bathrooms and children's rooms will acquire an instant sense of discreet charm.

Far left: Decorated and furnished in the palest shades of pink, mauve and green, this little sitting room has the delicate grace of a summer wedding cake. Elegant furniture designs in decorative metalwork and gilded wood add the finishing touch.

Left: Soft pinks and greens are used for this hand-painted lampshade, and the simple painted table provides a background of natural leaf green.

jasmine & honeysuckle

Some flowers are better known for their scent than their colour, but that doesn't make them any less generous in providing decorating inspiration. The creamy white blossom that smothers jasmine and honeysuckle at the height of summer has a subtlety that is more usable than many brighter blooms, and its delicate pink accents – seen in the jasmine buds before they open, and tinting the edges of the honeysuckle petals – add a warmer, faintly rosy glow. Almost edible in their delicious richness, these are the shades where the Flowers & Blossom palette comes closest to the Kitchen Garden palette (see page 106), with the simplicity of a country dairy and the coolness of buttermilk. There's nowhere these colours won't work, as long as you take care not to drown out their quiet tones with bold furnishings. Their softness is their strength, and you will lose that calming quality if you try to add bold contrasts or dramatic flourishes.

Below: A display of pink and white china lines the shelves of this painted cabinet, creating a light, summery feel in a traditional sitting room.

Right: Mixed pillows and cushions piled up in a country bedroom capture the delicate colours of jasmine and honeysuckle in a collection of different fabrics.

○ Layer whites and creams together: this will create more depth of tone and greater interest than using either shade individually.

○ Don't add colour to the mix, other than the naturally occurring accents of pink and occasional touches of soft green.

○ Avoid harsh contrasts such as dark wood, which will look jarring and break up the smoothness of this creamy scheme.

○ The colours are very soft and absorbent so you could benefit from adding occasional reflective surfaces such as glazed cupboards, lustreware or mother-of-pearl cutlery.

○ Look for pretty floral-sprigged fabrics in twining patterns that reflect the way honeysuckle grows.

KITCHEN GARDEN

KITCHEN GARDEN

FULL OF OLD-FASHIONED CHARM and farmhouse nostalgia, the colours of the kitchen garden are good enough to eat. Not confined to fruit and vegetables, they also reflect the delicious coolness of the dairy and the larder. Here you'll find the natural shades of strawberries and cream, Granny Smith apples, salad leaves and fresh chopped herbs, echoed in traditional country furnishings, like red and white linen, creamware crockery and green and cream tiles. More dramatic accent colours include the purple of plums, figs and aubergines; and the gold of pumpkins, squash, courgette flowers and Seville orange marmalade. This is a homely, simple palette celebrating old-fashioned traditions of domesticity. It has a functional feel that adapts well to different rooms, so there's no need to restrict the colours to kitchen furnishings. Surprisingly versatile, these colours can shift from soft and creamy to sharp and zesty, from cool and fresh to rich and buttery. Take inspiration from the glowing jars of preserves lined up on the larder shelf, with their gingham jam-pot lids and labels hand-written on creamy parchment; the jewel-bright beads trimming muslin food covers; and the soft, silvery greens of bunches of fresh, home-grown herbs hung up to dry.

Right: Silver-green herbs, translucent layers of crisp onion and the mellow creamware of kitchen crockery conjure up the colours of a country pantry.

THE KITCHEN GARDEN PALETTE

These ten shades provide a basic palette for recreating the colours found in the farmhouse kitchen and its adjoining vegetable garden. Soft dairy creams and crisp, crunchy whites provide plenty of easy-to-mix neutrals, with stronger colours coming from bright summer fruits, mellow leafy greens and occasional splashes of dark, dramatic aubergine or beetroot. Keep your scheme relatively limited so that the effect is fresh and simple, like the domestic setting that inspired it. Use this palette to help you plan your initial colours, then draw in other variations from the combinations shown on the following pages.

radish heart

Crisp, pure white – almost an absence of colour but, as a contrast to all the creams and bright reds of this palette, providing essential highlights in a cool neutral. Use it in layers with vanilla and buttermilk to offset their warmer tones, to keep the greens clean and fresh if they risk appearing murky, and to create fresh, simple schemes with bright tomato or raspberry.

vanilla

A very pale, slightly pink-tinged shade of cream perfect for creating softer highlights than pure white, but with enough depth of its own to act as a mellow background colour or a gentle contrast to deeper tones. A traditional dairy shade, it mixes naturally with raspberry pinks and pea greens and can be layered with other creams and whites for a subtle combination.

buttermilk

The richest of the creams, with much more yellow in it. It can become rather sickly if used on its own, so add plenty of cooler, whiter accents, or use it in combination with the pinks and greens of the palette. For extra interest, look for fabrics that provide the colour in a natural form and with plenty of texture, such as unbleached calico, loose-woven butter muslin and crinkly cheesecloth.

courgette flower

The golden yellow of the trumpet-shaped courgette flower. It contrasts beautifully with the fresh leaf greens and darker vegetation of the kitchen garden. Also the colour of pumpkins and squashes, and of jewel-bright marmalades lined up on larder shelves, it adds a warmer, more luxurious note than the pale creams, and echoes the harvest shades of the Field & Hedgerow palette (page 18).

sage

A delicate, silvery green with a hint of blue in it, making it much cooler than the rest of the palette. Subtle and versatile, sage is a restful background colour, soft and refreshing in bathrooms, bedrooms and sitting rooms, and the sort of shade you can live with almost anywhere. It has a closer affinity with the Sun, Sea & Sky palette (page 48) than with most other leaf greens.

lettuce

A bright leaf green, crisp and full of energy, yet cool and refreshing – somehow managing to stimulate and to calm the spirit at the same time. If it feels too strong to use as a background colour, try it for cushions and curtains (it's a delightful shade for summer cottons and linens), and mix it with floral pinks and blues as a change from the Kitchen Garden palette.

tomato

A bright, cheerful red, typical of kitchen linens and country ginghams. Useful for practical kitchens and playrooms, and for creating settings with Scandinavian or American folk-style simplicity. Mix it with crisp radish-heart whites to cool down the warm colour, and add touches of pink-tinged raspberry for a softer, prettier effect.

raspberry

A deep berry pink, deliciously pretty and full of summer flavour. It has plenty of subtlety, which makes it surprisingly usable. Best shown off by pale creams and yellows, it also mixes well with the gentle greens of the palette. Add plenty of textural variety – crushed velvets, shimmery silks and soft woollens – to reflect the contrasts within the fruit itself.

cabbage

A deep, old-fashioned green, traditionally mixed with creams and whites, and also sympathetic to browns and russets. It has a muted, comfortable feel that works well in studies and libraries with old leather furniture, worn tapestries, antique needlepoint fabrics and faded velvets. Use it to add an instant air of antiquity and to maintain a solid, welcoming atmosphere throughout living areas.

aubergine

The surprise element in the palette – a deep, moody purple that adds unexpected drama but mixes well with creams, greens and golds. Use it sparingly, so that it has real impact where it appears, but enjoy the sense of luxury and indulge in touches of gilt or gold alongside it, to bring out its opulent character.

Far left: The deep pink of redcurrants and raspberries creates splashes of bright colour against a buttermilk background. These shades are so potent that sparing use is all that's needed.

Centre left: The bright cherry colour of these traditional kitchen linens and the old-fashioned enamelware is softened by walls and furniture in vanilla cream, so that the overall effect is a gentle tone of pink rather than red.

Left: Dark plum is lightened by brighter touches of raspberry pink in this country kitchen, where the simple pine furniture and neat chequered floor create an old-fashioned atmosphere.

Above: A bowl of tulips beautifully combines the colours of raspberries and cream against a vanilla background.

Left: This earthenware pitcher and milk jug have the chunky practicality of a traditional farmhouse dairy, and the plain glaze in shades of buttermilk and clotted cream reinforces the simple, casual style of the table setting.

Below: Pale sage cabinets and cream walls provide a mellow setting for this homely kitchen. Traditional linens patterned with bands of cherry red and dark cabbage green add stronger colour against the plain stripped furniture.

Right: The mixed greens of herbs and spices create a subtle palette of decorating inspiration. Here, the pale green of fennel seeds is tinged with a golden glow against the pure white of the porcelain pestle and mortar.

Far right: Soft, creamy paint shades work as comfortably in bathrooms as in kitchens, especially in combination with traditional wood panelling and neat, scrubbed floorboards.

Below right: The gentle combination of green and cream, reminiscent of 1930s tiles and the dark leaves surrounding a head of crisp cauliflower, can be freshened with highlights of pure white and even gilded for a more luxurious effect.

Below far right: The herb garden is a source of softer, subtler greens. Silvery sage works particularly well for painted furniture, its pale colour cool and light-reflective. To create a leaf design on the background tone, use a laurel or bayleaf stencil and brush with a lighter shade of cream or mint green.

Left: Cream enamel and green-glazed china combine the fresh, summery feel of the kitchen garden with the mellow colours of the traditional larder. Blue and white may be the classic choice for tableware, but green and cream have their own nostalgic charm.

Below: A faded country-house sitting room decorated in deliciously edible shades of raspberries and cream, with hints of plum and gooseberry adding deeper accents.

Right: The larder supplies its own palette of whites and creams, perfect for layering one on top of another in subtle decorating schemes.

Far right: The creamy yellow curtains and covers of this tranquil bedroom are flecked with touches of raspberry pink and deeper flashes of bold colour.

radish heart & tomato

○ Use paint to revamp old furniture for a neat red and white scheme, and paint floorboards white to provide a clean, fresh background.

○ Keep the emphasis on white rather than red, using touches of bold colour to add contrast and definition.

○ Look for simple fabrics that reflect the practicality of the colours – ginghams, stripes and small floral sprigs are ideal.

Kitchen garden colours tend to fall into two distinct categories – the mellow wholesomeness of creams and greens, and the crisper, crunchier shades, which are energetic, invigorating and generally more refreshing. Red and white ginghams or striped linen tea towels, bright painted furniture and cheerful appliances in primary colours all reflect a no-nonsense mood that cuts through the gentle, earthy tones of traditional country furnishings.

Slice into a bunch of fresh garden radishes, and the contrast of crisp white centre against the crimson outer skin is startling. Add the brighter, orangey red of tomato, and the result is slightly warmer, but still very bold. This is a sharp, uncompromising mix, its strength coming from its simplicity. You can't dilute the scheme with pastels,

neutrals or half-shades – these colours demand to be used as they are – but despite their briskness, they are surprisingly versatile. As well as being perfect for country kitchens and bathrooms, their down-to-earth quality can create neat, uncluttered sitting rooms and bright, cheerful bedrooms.

The beauty of working with such uncomplicated colours is that they allow you a little more freedom in adding accessories. Where prettier shades run the risk of becoming frilly and overblown, the simplicity of a red and white scheme won't be undermined by the occasional decorative lampshade or floral-sprigged pillowcase. Lace, braid and broderie anglaise will add softer touches without looking fussy, and country-style details will be perfectly at home in a red and white kitchen.

Left: Crisp white towels trimmed with red ric-rac braid add a neat touch in kitchens and bathrooms. White linens are smart and traditional and provide a fresher look than mixed colours do.

Right: A checked cupboard lining matches the linen-bound notebooks and picks up the colours of the red and white china.

Opposite: Mismatched chairs and junkshop finds can be freshened up with a quick coat of paint to suit your kitchen colour scheme. Bright red gadgets and enamel storage containers add a practical, cheerful feel, while plain white tableware has an everyday simplicity that always looks right.

rosemary & sage

The colours of the herb garden are so distinctive that you can almost smell them. Gentle and soporific or fresh and tangy, they each have their own character, and the subtlety to work in almost any country setting. Among the most usable shades are soft, silvery sage, with its velvet leaves and mellow fragrance, and the steely blue-green of the rosemary bush. Naturally calming, they mix beautifully with greys, mauves and all kinds of blues – from the unexpected bright blooms of borage and sweet rocket, to the haze of flowers that hovers above a patch of lavender. Slate floors and worktops, the dull sheen of pewter, the cool glow of chrome and aluminium kitchen appliances – they all bring out the best in pale herb greens. Combine them with warm cream tiles or bright white paintwork, and see how these subtle colours create a restrained, elegant background wherever you use them. Halls, sitting rooms, kitchens and studies will all respond beautifully to their quiet, light-reflective quality. If you want to add stronger accents, look for furniture in dark, purply brown wood, which will provide plenty of contrast while maintaining the cool tone of the overall scheme.

Left: A little painted table holds a jug of mixed greenery and smoky-blue flowers, providing accents of slightly darker green against the pale apple-coloured wall.

Right: A tranquil kitchen in the softest of sage greens, with touches of light blue paintwork on the panelling above the worktops. Even the sleek modern appliances can't undermine the mellow, old-fashioned feel of this gentle colour scheme.

○ Maintain the pale, almost neutral colour scheme by avoiding bright colours – restrict accent shades to the natural blues and purples of herb flowers.

○ Add plenty of cool neutrals – marble worktops and washstands, stoneware containers and white china.

○ Use the combination in rooms that adjoin the garden, so that you bring outdoor colours into the house and reflect the shades of trees and foliage.

○ Use it to open up small rooms. The pale colours are light-reflective and space-making, and are softer than bright white.

raspberries & cream

○ Indulge in the romance of these easy, restful colours. Even people who wouldn't normally go for pink will find them amazingly usable.

○ Start by concentrating on the cream element of the colour scheme, adding sparing amounts of raspberry to see what effect it creates. Once you can gauge the balance, you'll be able to introduce more colour confidently.

○ Experiment with different strengths of colour, from the palest pastel tints to deeper, juicier shades that add more drama.

○ Be prepared to vary the shade of the cream you use – some yellowy creams may start to look rather sickly, whereas cool vanilla will have a lighter, fresher effect.

The most delicious of combinations, this romantic, summery mix is also one of the easiest to use. It is the sort of colour scheme that works in kitchens and bathrooms as effectively as in bedrooms and sitting rooms; that suits bright, south-facing rooms as well as gloomier settings; and that can be warm and comforting as well as cool and refreshing. Raspberry is a surprisingly subtle shade, its deeper tones rich and glowing like the centre of the fruit itself, but with a paler, softer quality, too, reflecting that velvety surface and fragile, crumbling texture. The addition of cream can either highlight the brightness of the pink, making it seem even fresher and crisper by contrast, or dilute it into a gentler blend, like juice and cream swirled together to create a pretty pastel. You have the choice of using these different shades individually to give the room a specific style, or combining them in mixed layers to provide a more complex colour scheme.

Below: Pink and white checks on an armchair create a pretty, inviting setting and provide gentle colour in this sun-filled sitting room.

Right: Deep raspberry pinks are layered with paler pastel bedcovers against cream-painted walls. The enamel jug on the windowsill shows the raspberry and cream colours swirled together on a single surface.

○ Mix different shades of green together, drawing inspiration from the colours and textures of the kitchen garden.

○ Use the darker colours to create calm and quiet in studies, or atmosphere and drama in formal dining rooms. The brighter, lighter shades will be refreshing in bathrooms, kitchens and bedrooms.

○ To vary the palette, add accents of lively yellows, cool blues and lilacs or striking raspberry pinks.

peapod & asparagus

Stronger, brighter greens can feel daunting to work with, until you accept that their natural quality makes them uniquely suited to creating comfortable furnishing schemes with timeless elegance. Where other colours can jar or pall, or look as though they had tried just a little too hard to create the right effect, green has a simple, organic quality and a refreshing, rejuvenating character that you won't easily tire of. Kitchen garden produce is a surprising source of colour inspiration, because it contains so many shades within its shoots and leaves. Look at the way the green of a leek or spring onion fades from dark to bright, then to pale and finally to white, providing a complete harmonizing colour palette as effectively as any paint chart. Now split open a broad-bean shell and see the crisp contrast between the bright shell, the soft white of the lining, and the row of pale beans nestling in it. Picture the combination as white woodwork against emerald-painted walls, or a glossy chequered splashback of green and white ceramic tiles, and see how fresh and clean the colours are. They are perfect for kitchens and bathrooms, and intriguing for the first impression they create in a hallway. Their invigorating spirit can also be put to good use in studies and libraries, and, indeed, wherever you want to encourage concentration and harness energy. Because different greens appear in a naturally random mix in the herb garden and vegetable patch, they seem to have a natural place alongside one another in interior schemes, too – and that comfortable partnership makes them easier to use as decorating colours than you might expect. Enjoy their sense of refreshing calm, and have fun experimenting with this unusual palette.

Left: Deep green walls and cool white woodwork create a quiet, calm workspace in this comfortable study. Flashes of brighter leaf and apple greens add a livelier, stimulating feel.

Above right: Bright green walls, as fresh as crisp peapods, glow in the sunlight of this hall window. Garden flowers reflect the colour in its purest form, highlighting the individual blues and yellows that combine to form the various shades of green.

Right: Handmade ceramic tiles, their uneven surfaces catching the light and dappling the colour, are fresh and summery in green and white.

aubergine & courgette flower

○ Be careful when choosing aubergine colours – avoid the hotter, crimson shades and stick to cool, smoky purples.

○ If you want a cooler, more restrained effect, add details in silver or pewter rather than in gold, and plenty of plain white paint and ceramics.

○ Don't try to add too much aubergine at once. This is a very potent colour and you need only a small quantity to produce a dramatic result.

Deep and dramatic, aubergine is one of those colours that can take on a life of its own once you let it loose in your home. Generally too overpowering for those of nervous disposition, and too bold to be used with safety if you're at all worried about what other people think, it has a strong, moody character that needs handling with care and restraint. Have faith in its richness, though, and you'll find it a fabulous source of luxury, capable of giving any room a distinctive air. It's particularly good for bedrooms and bathrooms – places where you want to indulge your senses, and where you can cope with colour schemes that you probably wouldn't want to live with 24 hours a day. Use it for satin bedcovers, crystal lamp droplets, lustreware and occasional areas of paintwork. For example, its use on the exterior of the old-fashioned free-standing bath pictured opposite has turned a spartan washroom into a relaxing retreat. You needn't go for over-the-top opulence – combining it with plain painted surfaces, natural wood, simple basketware and mellow, well-used furniture will balance the drama of the colour and make the whole room feel comfortable rather than luxurious.

Don't let the deep purple tones become gloomy or oppressive: the bright gold of pumpkins, squashes, fresh courgette flowers and marmalade makes a perfect companion to aubergine, emphasizing its natural richness but at the same time providing sunnier highlights. Yellow-orange paint colours and fabrics can both be used to good effect, while gold leaf and gilded details will add even more drama. Look for gilt mirror and picture frames, or rub old wooden frames with touches of gilt cream, and fit old brass door handles rather than sleek new chrome or steel. Your aim should be to keep the colour scheme romantic, and perhaps just a touch exotic. If the gold feels too bright, add touches of soft green, too – the colour of the aubergine stalk and courgette leaves. Green works beautifully with purple, and creates a quieter, more natural effect.

Right: The dark purple exterior of this bath gives the whole room a sense of luxury, even though the dramatic colour is offset by simple accessories and plain painted floorboards.

Below: Ripe figs capture the subtle moodiness of the colour scheme, as the green skin of the young fruit gives way to mature purple.

kale & cauliflower

A love-it-or-hate-it sort of colour, green hasn't always been the most popular of decorating shades. But there's a restful, comforting feel about its old-fashioned character, and the natural leaf shades of the kitchen garden translate very effectively into furnishing and paint colours. To see how these colours work together, look at the way individual fruits and vegetables combine harmonious shades in a single surface, as in the light veining that runs through the brighter green of kale or cabbage, or the pale creaminess of cauliflower florets against the darker leaves surrounding them.

Left: Deep green paint defines this bedroom's shape and architectural detail, creating a harmonious contrast with the pale green walls.

Below: The old-fashioned colours are perfectly suited to classic porcelain, especially with gilt decoration.

○ There's a slight risk of greens looking institutional. To avoid associating the colour with schools or hospitals, add touches of crisp white to freshen the scheme, or rich gold to lend a sense of luxury.

○ Take advantage of the schoolroom feel and use its practical, industrious character to provide a good working environment in your study or office.

○ Use it in old-fashioned kitchens, to conjure up utility style and a dairy feel, adding plenty of chunky cream china, simple enamel and practical wooden accessories.

○ Pick up the richer creams for a more indulgent effect in sitting rooms and dining rooms, and add touches of gold to make it feel more elegant.

125

gooseberry & buttermilk

○ Occasional touches of other clean, fresh berry colours – eg, red-checked kitchen linens – will add brighter accents.

○ Darker greens added sparingly will help to 'anchor' the scheme with more definition if the pale gooseberry colour is looking too thin and acidic.

○ For more dramatic accents, try touches of deep purply blues and reds. Gooseberries are close in tone to white grapes, so envisage the combination of black and white grapes together and aim for a similar contrast.

○ Pick up on the natural, leafy quality of the colour and mix it with other earth tones, or try shades from the Field & Hedgerow palette (see page 18).

Gooseberries are an acquired taste – sharp and unexpected in flavour, and not presenting such a dainty dish as the traditionally pretty summer berries. Whereas pinks and reds instantly suggest sweetness and romance, the pale yellow-green of the gooseberry is less immediately appealing. What brings it to life, both as a flavour and a colour, is the addition of cream, which enriches its texture and softens its acid tones into something deliciously subtle and tangy. This light, almost luminous shade has a greeny-gold glow that blends gently into muted, neutral country settings, contributing a hint of colour without trying to dominate the whole

scheme. The colour combination is especially good in kitchens, where the natural creaminess mixes well with old-fashioned fittings and scrubbed paintwork, and in studies and libraries, where its understated colour suits the quiet setting and contrasts gently with the worn leather of old books and furniture. Try it in garden rooms, too, where the dappled sun that filters through the trees outside will pick up the yellow tones and add sparkling highlights. And use it for rubbed or distressed paintwork, layering greens and yellows together so that the broken finish reflects the translucent colour of the fruit.

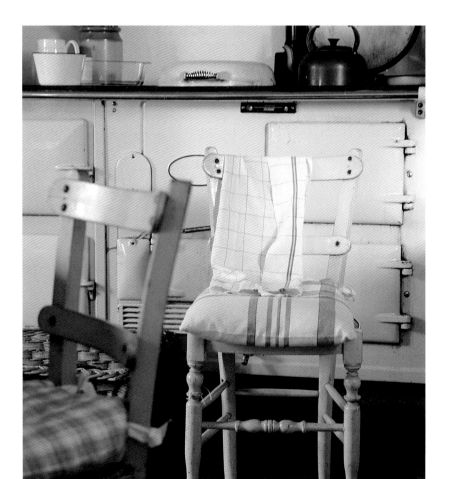

Left: The yellowy green paintwork of the kitchen chairs stands out against the softer, creamier colour of the Aga behind. The shift in tone is very subtle, but the chairs have a sharper, cleaner note.

Right: The faded, streaky green of the bookcase suits the comfortably studious air of the room, with mellow cream walls and just a touch of stronger, deeper colour in the paintwork of the distant door.

strawberry, apple & mint

○ Keep the greens fresh and pale: too strong a colour may be hard to live with and will create a very harsh contrast with the red.

○ Avoid having too much natural wood that might dull the colours and lead to a 'muddy' mix. Go for painted woodwork that will freshen and lighten the scheme.

○ Keep the furniture light and graceful, opting for carved wood and wrought-iron designs rather than chunkier pieces whose solid shape could make the colour scheme feel heavy or overpowering.

The unmistakable combination of the classic Pimms mix, this is a scheme that is redolent of summer. Creamy white, like a sliced apple, the mixed greens of apple and mint leaves and the fresh red of cut strawberries provide the perfect blend of crisp, cool colours. The contrasting shades balance each other beautifully, so that no single one predominates, with the cooler greens offsetting the splashes of bright red, and clean whites preventing the green from appearing too muted or grey. Strong greens and reds can fight if used too liberally together, but if you stick to pale mint, sage or mossy tones, and mix them with pink-tinged berry reds, the combination will stay crisp, fresh and easy to live with. You may be able to find a fabric or wallpaper that incorporates both colours on a cream or white background – floral patterns will provide the right colour mix if you can't find fruit designs. Otherwise, try experimenting with contrasting paintwork, either using details in one colour to add accents to a larger area of the other, or picking out details in red and green in a predominantly neutral room.

Left: Fresh white paintwork offsets the pale mint green walls, while accents of bright strawberry red highlight the bedcover and ceiling beams in this summery bedroom.

Right: A delicate pink and green scalloped border, hung with tiny fabric beads, trims this cream linen lampshade and adds a pretty, Victorian-style finish to the green-painted base.

129

SLATE & STONE

SLATE & STONE

THE MOST ELEGANT OF COUNTRY COLOURS, these nearly neutral shades work as a muted version of stronger schemes. Blues and mauves fade into gentle grey; pinks and yellows bleach into soft beige or sand. The effect is like an old photo, mellow and timeless, with an organic quality that feels very natural and provides a perfect backdrop for country life. The cool greys of slate and charcoal, the warmer tones of clay, terracotta and sandstone, and the pretty shades provided by delicately veined marble will all provide subtle inspiration for furnishing colours, as well as supplying actual materials for you to incorporate in your home. Texture becomes increasingly important if you are working with predominantly neutral shades, so this chapter includes ideas for different surfaces that will accent contrasts and create interesting depth and shadow. Make the most of natural, textured fabrics such as linen, hessian and corduroy, renovate traditional slate and flagstone floors, and enjoy the variegated, uneven tone of wall finishes such as raw plaster and exposed brickwork. Plain white ceramics and pale, creamy terracotta shades will provide gentle highlights against the darker, muddier shades. Accessories can be kept to a minimum: the beauty of this look is its simplicity.

Right: A stone-coloured linen napkin, trimmed with rough-textured shells to weight the fabric, creates a practical food cover for a country kitchen.

THE SLATE & STONE PALETTE

These ten shades provide a neutral palette that recreates the colours of the countryside's natural materials. The subtle tones are wonderfully satisfying to use because they let you build up layers of character and contrast without swamping the room with any definite sense of colour. Look for a good balance of warm and cool shades, and keep the different whites handy to add gentle highlights so that the scheme doesn't become muddy. Use this palette to plain your basic colours, then create your own subtle effects by drawing in variations from the combinations shown on the following pages.

alabaster

A pale porcelain white, which is clean, light-reflective and almost translucent. It creates an elegant background colour for graceful, decorative furnishings, and will add delicate highlights if used for woodwork and details. Fine china and white enamel can supply it in the form of tableware, and crisp linen provides softer lines. Layer it with warmer whites and creams for a richer effect.

limestone

A warmer, more textured white, comfortable as a background shade and easy to supply with paintwork, fabric, furniture and ceramics. This is the sort of colour that works comfortably on uneven surfaces and panelled walls, where its mellow tone gives a simple, rustic feel. It makes a good contrast with wooden beams and floorboards and with other natural materials.

sandstone

A soft, pale yellow, beautifully warm but with a hint of cool grey that tones down any tendency to brightness. It will provide a stronger sense of colour when used against completely neutral shades, but is still subtle enough to keep the overall effect restrained and understated. Sandstone works particularly well in combination with balancing greys and natural slate blues.

marble

The palest of greys, a silvery shade that's barely more than white darkened by shadow, but that can also provide sparkling highlights of its own. A good alternative to white for woodwork and painted furniture, it works well for soft, matt fabrics such as wool and felt, and adds a delicate shimmer to silks, velvets and sheer voiles. Use it to cool down an over-bright white room.

putty

Muted and mutable, a subtle grey-brown shade that seems able to adapt to surrounding colours and surfaces with little effort. It sometimes seems to have a pinkish chocolatey bloom: at other times, it can appear as a cooler grey. An easy background colour to live with, it's also very versatile for woodwork and can be readily found in neutral fabrics such as corduroy, linen and hessian.

clay

A warm, rustic colour that provides a range of shades perfect for country furnishings. Rich and earthy, it is generally best suited to simple fabrics such as woollens and corduroys, but it can take on a more luxurious look if used for velvets and chenilles. It also supplies effective texture, in hand-thrown ceramics and unfinished wood surfaces, giving country rooms a robust, practical feel.

terracotta

Similar to clay, but usually veering slightly towards the redder tones. Like clay, it can conjure up a range of shades and effects, but the overall feel is hotter and drier, sometimes giving a powdery look. Almost a deeper version of plaster pink, it is tremendously comfortable, has subtle depth and is good for recreating sun-bleached, Mediterranean styles.

granite

An imposing shade, dark and solid, but warmer than the undiluted grey tones because it incorporates an element of reddish brown. It can provide a rich sense of drama and atmosphere and works particularly well in sophisticated, tailored schemes with a more contemporary feel. Don't overdo it, or the strong colour will feel too oppressive, but use small quantities with greys and whites.

slate

A mid-grey with plenty of character. Far more definite than marble, slate is good for supplying strength and atmosphere when set against softer, paler colours. It becomes calm and restful if used to balance warm reds and yellows. Make the most of its austere, down-to-earth quality by combining it with Shaker-style furnishings and simple, understated colour schemes.

charcoal

The drama queen of the Slate & Stone palette – a deep, moody tone with just a hint of purple. Dark and leaden, it creates wonderful shadows and striking focal points, yet its inky, blue-black nature also works beautifully in intricate monochrome patterning on fabrics and wallpapers. Cool and classic, it's the colour to call on when you want to make an effortless impact.

135

Above: The old brickwork and weathered wood of this doorway have faded to the same soft, muted shade, creating a warm, sunlit entrance to the cottage. Somewhere between grey and brown, it has a gentle honeyed appearance.

Right: A bleached grey cabinet is filled with ochre-coloured ceramics, combining warm and cold neutrals together against the rich timbers of the polished floorboards.

Far right: Moody greys and browns create a formal, dramatic sitting room with classical touches – an elegantly curved pitcher on a table, and a bust on the windowsill, contrasting with the simpler plaid cushions and painted wood.

Far left: Grey-blue walls the colour of faded slate are cool and elegant. Here, heavy cream curtains and cream woodwork provide neat, understated highlights.

Left: Pale grey paintwork gives this side table and cabinet a Scandinavian-style finish, with plain wood worktops and handles maintaining the simple farmhouse look and adding warmer tones.

Above: Painting the interior of the cupboard a warm chocolate brown to contrast with the slate blue doors creates an earthy Shaker-style effect. Plain and patterned stoneware adds monochrome detailing.

Right: The checked chair-cover provides a single flash of colour against neutral creams and greys.

Far left: Deep sepia tones are light and elegant when used in delicate toile de Jouy patterns, adding just a touch of drama against a cool white and cream background. Plain white linen and ceramics create the simplest of table settings, with cream-painted woodwork giving the scheme a little more depth and richness.

Left: The faintest pink blush lifts these almost-white flowers out of the neutral background of the windowsill.

Below left: Muted stone colours acquire more character when painted onto woodwork panelling, so that the shadows create areas of light and dark, giving the surface accent and definition. Fabrics in different textures add more depth and interest.

Below right: Different shades of white add their own highlights against the pale grey walls of this tranquil bedroom. The painted furniture contributes a layer of deeper tone, so that the only pure colour is the pink fabric of the lampshade.

❍ Think of slate and sandstone as diluted versions of blue and yellow and use them to create subtler effects – contented rather than happy, restful rather than refreshing.

❍ Adjust the balance between the two colours according to whether you want to cool down or warm up the setting. Extra sandstone will be brighter and sunnier; extra slate will tone down strong sunlight.

❍ Look for natural materials that repeat the colours. Pewter and gunmetal accessories will supply additional greys, while wood, basketware and exposed brickwork will emphasize the sandstone shades.

❍ Introduce occasional highlights of pure white china or linen for a fresher, brighter effect.

slate & sandstone

Left: Pale sandstone walls and a wood-planked floor create a mellow background for slate-grey kitchen cabinets.

Below: Here, the two shades combine for a rustic effect.

Below right: Grey gingham fabric and a striped throw echo the cool woodwork in this pretty yellow morning room, softening the glare of the sun.

The beauty of neutral schemes is the way that warm and cool tones balance each other naturally without the need for obvious colour. Shadowy slate grey and the soft creamy ochre of sandstone are a perfect mix because of this balance – wonderfully mellow, but with enough variety and contrast to create essential depth and atmospheric shadows. Look at the grey tones that appear on a sandy-yellow wall when the light leaves it, and you can see how comfortably the two shades enhance one another, the darker colour drawing out the natural character of the lighter one. The same is true of grey surfaces where sunlight touches them, gilding their sombre mood with a layer of warmth.

The rich glow of a wooden worktop against a slate-grey cabinet is enough to conjure up the effect. A slab of slate set on top of an ochre-painted cupboard behaves in a similar way. Strengthened into blue and gold, these colours would have the invigorating freshness of the Sun, Sea & Sky palette, but diluted into this muted form, they become gentle and restful – shades that you can live with every day, that provide a practical backdrop to kitchens and through-traffic hallways, and that are pretty enough to create elegant sitting and dining rooms. Use them as an alternative to brighter blues and yellows, and try them if you want a neutral effect without losing all sense of colour.

putty & limestone

The subtlest neutrals manage to convey a sense of texture along with their colour. The bleached, chalky look of limestone white – soft and powdery, sometimes with a green tinge reminiscent of moss, lichen and natural weathering – produces this effect. The chocolatey grey-browns of putty shades are similarly expressive, pale and velvety like moleskin, with hints of silvery pink that catch the light beautifully. Use these colours in combination with elegantly carved furniture and delicate crystal accessories, and you create a cool, restrained setting in which the muted neutrals are highlighted by a frosting of white accents. The simplicity of the palette lends itself to textured plain linen fabrics,

rough hessians and understated Shaker-style checks, but its pale delicacy is also perfect for prettier, daintier fabrics, like coffee-coloured lace, beaded oyster silks and crisp, white broderie anglaise. Echo the tracery of lace with intricate, filigree wallpaper designs, and with jacquard or damask fabric weaves in which a pale pattern lifts itself out of a tonal background. Hang panels of embroidered voile at the window to increase this subtle tone-on-tone effect. The key to this combination is its softness, so you need to keep the finish mellow. Stick to pale white or cream walls and woodwork, with painted or limed-wood furniture and stripped wood floors or natural matting.

○ This combination will produce a different effect depending on the accents you add – use cream for a gentle, mellow contrast or white for a fresher look.

○ Use these sophisticated colours to add elegance to a small room, keeping the background mostly pure white or cream, with putty-coloured accents ensuring that the effect is restrained and down to earth.

○ Add plenty of texture to enrich the mix and give the simple colours a sense of warmth and comfort.

○ Avoid darker woods which would create too strong a contrast.

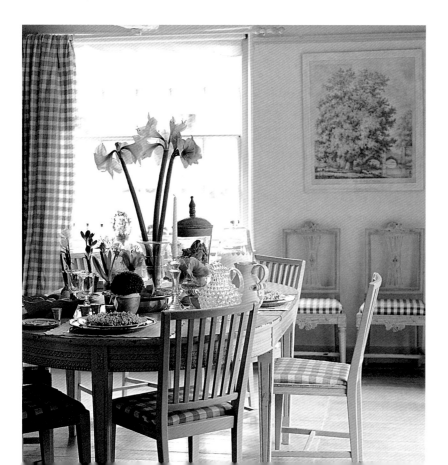

Left: Painted furniture and simple checked fabrics provide mellow putty tones against the limestone white background. A table set with crystal and white china adds sparkling highlights.

Right: A delicate tracery of white highlights the coffee-coloured wallpaper, with white panelling and paintwork adding its own details and shadows. Layered covers in creams, whites and putty shades are piled on the elegant carved bed.

plaster & terracotta

If you are looking for warmth and richness among your neutrals, you need materials that provide plenty of variety within their basic shades. Raw plaster is one of the most subtle, a mellow mushroom pink that changes shade as it dries, creating a stippled surface full of inspiring tones. Terracotta is even more versatile, with tiles ranging from pale biscuit cream, through pinks and oranges to deep burgundy-browns, depending on the colour of the original clay. Use these ready-made palettes to pick shades that harmonize naturally, either keeping to a narrow range of plaster pinks and beiges for an earthy, unfinished look, or incorporating stronger contrasts of cream and orange for more drama. Look for tweed and plaid fabrics that weave the colours into a gentle mix, or use mottled terracotta for a tiled floor or wall that combines different depths of tone in a single surface. Details in cream or gold will enrich the effect even more – or, if the look is too warm for comfort, cool it down with slate blues and greys or cool metals such as chrome and steel.

○ New plaster always needs to dry completely before it can be painted or papered over, so you have plenty of time to decide whether you like the raw effect, and to draw inspiration from its changing shades.

○ Remember that the colour of terracotta will change as it weathers or if you seal it.

Far left: A plain wooden worktop and mosaic-effect terracotta tiles are rich and earthy against walls the colour of raw plaster.

Left: Slate grey cushions add a cooler, darker tone to pale walls stippled in soft mushroom pink.

Right: A woollen throw in checks of pink and grey casts a layer of comfortable warmth over this armchair.

○ Look for fabrics and soft textures in the same two shades so that the colours aren't confined to the hard surfaces.

147

charcoal & granite

○ Use metal furniture and finishes to provide elements of charcoal colour – pewter lamp bases and tableware, black-leaded fire grates, wrought-iron furniture and curtain poles.

○ Make the most of natural wood to give the scheme structure. Ceiling beams, solid, rustic furniture and heavy planked doors will all add definition.

○ Look for materials that will supply natural rich browns and dark reds, such as leather furniture and the darker shades of terracotta floor tiles.

○ Keep the background light and plain, and add the darker colours in details so that they don't seem overpowering or gloomy.

○ This is a strong colour combination, so stick to plain surfaces and simple patterns to keep the effect understated and elegant.

Stone colours lose their 'neutral' identity tag once you move into the deeper, darker shades. Sombre greys and browns, their intense tones creating instant focal points, are never going to fade into the background or be taken for granted. Introducing them to a scheme promises drama and atmosphere, for these colours have a sense of character that demands to be taken seriously. Dark charcoal grey is particularly versatile, with a cool, purply quality that sets moody shadows against lighter shades. Try it in contrasting materials, mixing shiny satins with soft, matt woollens so that you recreate the way the light plays on the different surfaces of charcoal – glinting on its smooth, sheared planes and being absorbed by the rougher sides. The severity of the colour is reminiscent of starchy Victorian restraint

and old-fashioned tailoring, but it also has a cool simplicity that adapts beautifully to contemporary style and plain, understated furnishings. Combine it with rough-textured wood and pale, chalky paint shades, and it acquires an almost unbeatable natural elegance, calm and sophisticated in sitting rooms and dining rooms, and quiet enough to use in bedrooms, too.

Granite supplies an additional quality of tone, its rugged solidity tempered by the mottled, flecked surface familiar from kitchen sinks and worktops. Sometimes grey, but often a dark brown or a pinkish red, it mixes comfortably with charcoal shades, accentuating their deeper tones, but providing a warmer, more textured feel that enriches the whole effect.

Left: Warm brown bedcovers add granite-flecked colour, with grey-green paintwork and grey-painted metal tables sounding a cooler note.

Right: Deep grey covers and cushions and the rich brown of the curtain provide a dramatic contrast with the white bedlinen and pale panelled wall, creating a sombre, sophisticated bedroom setting.

marble & flint

Two of the prettiest forms of stone combine here for a colour scheme of subtle variety and gentle contrasts. The beauty of both these materials is the way they incorporate both warm and cool tones within their intriguing surfaces – the veining in a slab of marble can drift from grey to pink, and a flint wall may well contain blues, corals and honey golds as well as the more expected blacks and greys. Take inspiration from these ready-made mixes, confident that the same shades will work comfortably together and that the neutral schemes they create will be full of interest and sparkle. Grey used on its own runs the risk of appearing cold and gloomy, but add touches of warmer pink or gold and the mood is instantly lifted. Honey-coloured wooden floorboards or furniture will lighten a grey-painted room, and pretty pastel fabrics will offset the severity of a grey marble fireplace. For more inspiration, take a look at the colours explored in the Sun, Sea & Sky chapter (see pages 44–71), and introduce some of the shades found among shells and pebbles to provide subtly warm accents.

○ Look at the way flint is combined with the golds and beiges of rounded pebbles in traditional house design, and use the same highlights to bring out the more colourful shades in the stone.

○ Degrees of warmth and cool are relative, so contrast different shades to see how they react. A soft blue will look warmer and prettier when set against a moody grey.

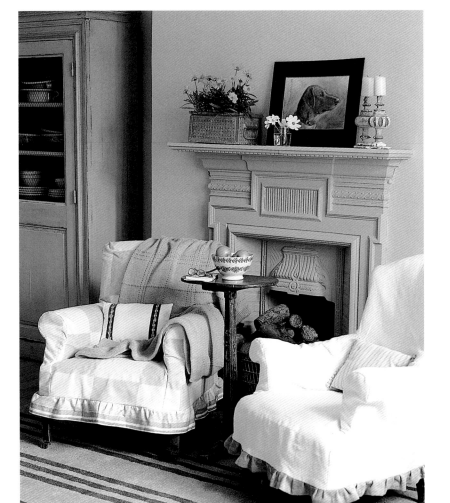

Far left: Pale blue walls and a grey and white painted floor give this landing a flint-cool air, but stripped wood furniture and gilded picture frames add warmer tones.

Left: This little sitting room emphasizes the pretty pinks and blues found in flint and marble, creating soft highlights against the austere grey wall.

Right: Honey-gold floorboards and coral-coloured shells contrast with the cool pale grey of the painted chair.

clay & limestone

Sometimes you want a richer mix than most neutrals are able to supply, which is where clay tones come in handy. Offering the same variety and versatility as terracotta, clay has the fuller, riper quality of the raw material, rather than the drier, crisper finish of the fired terracotta colours. From pale porcelain creams to rich dark browns, it can also throw up red-golds and muddy greys, depending on the consistency of the earth it's made from and the metals it contains. This robust palette lets you create stronger, more dramatic schemes, setting light shades beside dark ones in moody contrasts, and adding warmer mid-tones for comfort. Natural wood can provide many of these hues – limed or bleached to create the paler tones, waxed or polished for greater depth. The chalky white of limestone will add brighter highlights in paintwork, linen and ceramics. For extra energy you can include flashes of bright orange, too, picking up on the richest clay accents and lifting the whole effect out of the purely functional with a layer of more flamboyant colour.

Left: The comfortable warmth of this country dining room is the result of a beautifully balanced colour mix, with rich clay tones providing a range of browns against the simple white-painted walls, chairs and floorboards, and cushions adding a flash of bright gold.

Right: Limestone white walls and pale limed floorboards create a cool background for darker, muddier browns and greys.

○ Limestone white is one of the most versatile background shades, especially on uneven surfaces and wood panelling or floorboards.

○ Use the full extent of the clay palette to add rich depth of colour with warm browns, golds and reds.

○ Use the brightest shades to add colourful accents to neutral schemes, balancing the stark contrast of dark against light with cheerful mid-tones for a livelier look.

○ Mix natural and painted woods for a comfortable, informal effect, rather than trying to make everything match.

○ Use these warm tones to enrich a cool, north-facing room, adding occasional touches of brighter white to keep the scheme fresh.

○ Combine them with clean lines and simple furnishings, letting the warmth of the colours soften the austere setting with mellow, welcoming comfort.

○ Pick up their richer tones in luxurious fabrics such as silks and velvets, and add touches of gilding in fine china and picture frames to give a more elegant effect.

○ If the clay shades feel too rich and earthy, shift the balance to increase the paler, sandstone element, so that the overall feel is creamy yellow with a few stronger accents.

sandstone & clay

The buttery warmth of these colours almost belongs in the dairy shades of the Kitchen Garden palette, but they have an earthy, muddy quality that is more in keeping with natural stone and soil. Simple enough to use in the most rustic setting, but with a richness equally well suited to elegant country drawing rooms, this is a combination to conjure up mellow, comfortable charm wherever you need it. The key to its restfulness is the lack of any bright highlights or dramatic contrasts. Instead, use natural wood, rush-seated furniture and woven coir matting on the floor to provide a background of muted warmth. Keep the paintwork to a narrow range of gentle honey shades, so that the room acquires a single overall colour tone rather than the ceilings and woodwork being picked out with a brighter white.

Let fabrics and furniture provide their own natural shadows, such as the narrow stripe of old-fashioned blankets, the graining and panelling of wood-work, or the outline of a decorative chair back or an iron-framed bed against the plain colour of the wall behind it. Look for fabrics that combine a subtle variety of shades in their patterns, such as muted stripes and plaids, or layer a plain silk or linen curtain with a lining in a deeper tone so that it provides contrast without becoming a distracting focal point. Gentle highlights can be added with parchment whites and warm creams, soft neutrals that add texture rather than light. And if the scheme becomes too rich for comfort, you can simply introduce a few elements of cool blues or metallic greys to tone down the warmth and restore the neutral balance.

Far left: Old-fashioned dormitory-style bed frames create stark outlines against the mellow sandstone wall. Traditional blankets and coir matting keep the effect warm but simple.

Left: The subtle stripes of the curtain pick up the different tones of the honey-coloured room: the soft yellow of the wall, the pale wood of the corner cabinet, and the darker wood of the little chair in the foreground.

chalk & graphite

This is a combination of clean contrasts, the darker blue-grey tones of natural graphite creating deep shadows against cool white. The expanse of pale, chalky background keeps the overall effect light, with patches of black, navy blue or dark grey adding accents and details. You may find these in fabrics patterns or paint colours, but they can also be supplied more subtly by natural materials such as metalwork or ebony, which will create elegant patterns and silhouettes. The resulting scheme is fresh and bright, although it may be too chilly for most north-facing rooms. The bright white may help to compensate for a lack of natural sunlight, but the effect will still be overwhelmingly cool. These understated colours have a close affinity with the nautical shades of the Sun, Sea & Sky palette (see page 48), so if you want to add a little more colour, rather than sticking to the predominantly neutral tones of Slate & Stone, you could consider introducing pinks and yellows to warm up the effect, or blues and greens to echo the natural greys and keep the room cool and fresh. Small touches are all that's necessary to enrich the mix and lift the combination out of its monochrome simplicity.

Left: Touches of grey-blue patterning on the fabric, a wooden picture frame and decorative wrought-iron handles on the chest of drawers provide occasional darker accents against the chalk-white walls, furniture and fabric.

Right: The dark stripes of the bed canopy and chair-cover are crisp and stark against the white-painted furniture, floorboards and foreground walls. The mid-grey of the far walls softens the contrast.

○ This combination works perfectly in simple checks and stripes, so look for fabrics such as old-fashioned mattress ticking, and gingham in navy and white or black and white.

○ For more ornament and a less nautical feel, seek out classical monochrome patterns such as toile de Jouy, providing detailed figurative images with a traditionally elegant feel.

○ Soften the restrained, understated effect of the colours with fabric flourishes such as bed drapes and canopies or architectural details like archways and alcoves.

○ To add warmth without introducing colour to the scheme, opt for a plain wood or terracotta floor.

INDEX

PHOTOGRAPHIC ACKNOWLEDGEMENTS

Caroline Arber pages 36 left, 52 top right, 108 left, 109 left, 109 right, 114 left, 122, 129, 153
Jan Baldwin pages 38, 78 right
Tim Beddow pages 31, 39
Mark Bolton page 125
Charlie Colmer pages 1, 21 right, 29, 35 left, 51 top right, 51 bottom right, 55, 64, 67, 70, 78 left, 79 top left, 81, 83 bottom, left, 88, 92, 95, 137 right, 138 left, 147 left, 155
Christopher Drake pages 110 bottom, 143 left, 154
Andreas von Einsiedel page 140 top right
Laurie Evans page 113 top left
Craig Fordham pages 47, 58
Kate Gadsby page 123
Georgia Glynn Smith pages 54 top right, 102-103
Catherine Gratwicke pages 24 bottom left, 33, 54 bottom, 56, 61 right, 133, 140 left, 141 left, 145
Gridley and Graves page 100
Scott Hawkins page 26
Huntley Hedworth pages 23 left, 32, 52 bottom, 65, 71, 138 right, 139 right, 141 right, 143 right, 150, 151 right
Ray Kachatorian page 11
Sandra Lane pages 42, 68
Tom Leighton pages 59, 84, 97, 126, 142, 156
Michael Luppino pages 2, 83 right, 148

Mark Luscombe White pages 24 bottom right, 66
Charles Maraia page 100
James Merrell pages 17, 20 top left, 20 right, 23 left, 23 right, 24 top left, 24 top right, 25, 28 left, 30, 34, 36 right, 37, 41, 44-45, 53 bottom, 54 top left, 57 right, 62, 63, 75, 80 top left, 80 top right, 86, 89, 91, 93, 111 bottom left, 112 top left, 112 bottom, 118, 121 bottom, 124, 127, 136 right, 144, 147 right, 149, 151 left
Tham Nhu Tran pages 43, 52 top left, 53 top left, 69, 72-73, 79 right, 85 left, 98, 115
Bridget Peirson pages 60, 61 left, 111 top left, 121 top
Nick Pope page 117
Alex Ramsay page 136 left
Steven Randazzo pages 5, 7
Kim Sayer pages 14-15
Bob Smith pages 8-9, 20 bottom left, 90, 128
Ron Sutherland page 23 right
Debi Treloar pages 35 right, 40, 57 left, 80 bottom, 108 right, 111 top right, 113 right, 114 right, 146
Pia Tryde pages 13, 28 right, 50 left, 82 left, 87, 96, 99, 110 top, 111 bottom right, 116, 120
Simon Upton pages 119, 139 left, 157
Peter Williams page 105
Peter Woloszynski page 22 left
Polly Wreford pages 51 top left, 94, 152